ALL THINGS WELL:
Helping
Youth
Discover
Their Open Door

ALL THINGS WELL:

Helping
Youth
Discover
Their Open Door

DR. CLARENCE ALSTON

Library of Congress Control Number:		2022903553
ISBN:	Hardcover	978-1-6698-1328-6
	Softcover	978-1-6698-1327-9
	eBook	978-1-6698-1326-2

Print information available on the last page.

Rev. date: 02/22/2022

To order additional copies of this book, contact:
Xlibris
844-714-8691
www.Xlibris.com
Orders@Xlibris.com
839429

I am grateful to my wife, Sylvia, for her clam assurance and for my family for encouraging me as I chase after my dreams.

Contents

CONTENTS

To The Reader:

Those who are adult by Chronological definition, must ponder how we were yesterday's tomorrow. But now our youth represent today's tomorrow. They plead to us, "Help Me Become All I was Created to Be!"

INTRODUCTION

In an earlier book titled, *Reclaiming Our Youth: A Call to Generational Responsibility*, I identified various lifestyles destructive to contemporary youth. I proposed that those lifestyles emanated from behaviors inherited via observation or reputation of their 20th century forebears. Essentially, the negative proclivities of 21st youngsters evolved from atrocious demonstrations of an earlier generation. This conclusion perhaps reflects a society which was more tolerant, accommodating offenders who were less inhibited. More succinctly, unhealthy behaviors of a previous generation devolved into indiscriminate conflict and unprovoked violence. Unsuspecting women were pushed toward the rail tracks of a moving train. Fragile, defenseless grandmothers have been savagely attacked with fists or hammers on a public sidewalk. Octogenarian veterans of several national wars were punched in the face and cast down to the cold, brutal concrete.

Parents, educators, psychologists and well - meaning politicians have funded and supported various attempts to bring about change. Conflict resolution programs, self-esteem guides and counseling strategies have provided negligible impact on the destruction perpetuated by individuals so young. The ruination persists across age groups, ethnicities, gender designations and economic groups.

This manual introduces a divergent understanding of the root causes and resolutions of this appalling waste of human potential. It is a waste because, inevitably, the perpetrators end up in the justice system, or worse, death by accident or revenge. It is my hope that this book provokes an urgent confrontation and discussion among parents and other concerned adults who touch the youth's lives. Perhaps these discussions will challenge all of us to analyze this affinity of contemporary youth toward violence, substance abuse and educational failure.

The difficulties addressing the obstacles are similar to those described in *Reclaiming Our Youth*. The urgency required to attack the problem and activate reliable solutions is still prominent. Some of the suggestions are familiar to those who have heard of *Reclaiming Our Youth*. Hopefully this update is relevant and useful.

There is a significant distinction between this book versus *Reclaiming our Youth*. One important difference is emphasis placed on individual young people. The individuals are the primary role players. They possess the power to implement change in themselves and others once they understand who they are as well as their responsibility. They have the responsibility to initiate change in their own thinking and behavior.

Previously, parents were challenged to reclaim their wayward young person. This presentation encourages parents and others to help the children become what God created them to be. If this can be achieved in a practical way, everything else will fall into place.

Numerous discussions about the destruction contemporary youth initiate or contribute to, despite the myriad view points about the future of contemporary youth or the future of American society in the hands of modern day youth, remains a focal point of concern. As mentioned, unlimited conflict resolution efforts and programs have manifested minimal impact on the downward spiral of negative behavior among the young and not so young. The plethora of issues are reflected in a representative number of the mature population as well. That contradiction must be addressed further in another discussion.

Suffice it to say that the destructive trend observed among young people can be adequately addressed if the spiritual condition, so prevalently ignored, is examined in a pragmatic fashion. Without questioning, providing assistance to youth to explore an effective spiritual journey will require adult leadership from adults already engaged in their own spiritual trek.

God has provided the means to offer guidance and blessings for our youth. The adult population is accountable to God if we fail to provide guidance. As communities, the country and the world, the adults may continue to reap infinite brokenness and despair if the wisdom of the Creator is not applied to the solution which is supposed to rescue His creation.

...For a great and effective door has opened to me....
I Corinthians 16: 9
NJKV

... see, before you I have set an open door; no one can shut it.
Revelations 3:8
NJKV

YOUTH MUST REALIZE THEIR IDENTITY

CREATED POTENTIAL

The term "youth" encompasses a broad group. It may designate those who are young chronologically or merely young at heart. This discussion refers to the persons who have not yet reached the age of twenty- one.

Throughout this discussion, I refer to parental or adult influence. I believe that guidance for youth relies on the influence someone is able to exert. Adults who have no influence on young people stand little chance of affecting the latter's thinking or behavior. Adults who fail to establish a meaningful, positive relationship with young people can dispense with the idea of developing an influential relationship. Effort is required and motive is essential as well. Young people tend to exercise special editing skills (the ability to decipher another person's attitude or feelings by observing nonverbal cues). These editing skills enable many young people in urban environments to survive by avoiding places and people who might pose danger. They are able to detect the motive or genuineness early in their contact with another individual. I re-emphasize that this unique skill frequently assists urban youngsters in avoiding unsafe or antagonistic community environments. They navigate with an objective of avoiding danger. Their safety frequently demands quick thinking and even speedier action or reaction.

Most young people expect honesty, consistency and loyalty from adults in their lives if any hope of influence is to survive. Generally, contemporary youth mature quite rapidly emotionally and socially. Their exposure to various stimuli and events occur quite early in their chronological existence. For that reason, positive relationships with a supportive adult must be established early as well. Early support from caring adults can help young people make productive decisions before it's too late. Often, current adult lifestyles make it difficult for them to carry out close physical supervision of young people. Activities of young people can remain obscured to the well-meaning adult in a youngster's life. This independence necessitates that the youngster possesses the proclivity and ability to make healthy decisions. They need to possess the motivation to act with an awareness of the long term and short term decisions which can impact their lives.

As adults, our greatest opportunity to influence young people may be the greatest contribution we can make to them. We need to help them develop a clear understanding of who they are, how important they are, and how responsible they are for making decisions consistent with who they are. They must realize the power of their own created potential. This identity may clarify their responsibility to maximize that potential. Job 12:3 says, *"To God belongs wisdom and power; counsel and understanding are His"*. Jeremiah 1:5-6 reminds young people *"Before I formed you in my womb I knew you; before you were born I set you apart; I appointed you as a prophet to the nations"*. God teaches Jeremiah that He is the Creator who designs the crown of His human creation with purpose, talents and skills to carry out that purpose. A purpose is predetermined, so are the attributes required to succeed and fully complete the mission. The Creator indicates the challenges or opposition His servants will face. In light of the omniscience of the creator all of us are are fully prepared for success and fulfillment in the life work we have been called to do. Our charge is to obey and follow directions. God does not hold Jeremiah responsible for the results. Jeremiah's task is to walk in faith and trust the sufficiency of the creator, *"Do not be afraid for I am with you and will rescue you"* declares the Lord.

Many young people desperately seek relief and consolation. They question why they exist. They ask, "What am I supposed to do with my life?" Frequently the responses from adults are confusing and evasive. Sadly, some of the adults are asking similar questions about their own lives. This uncertainty can be frustrating and frightening to a youngster. In frustration and hopelessness, too many young people seek relief via destructive behavior such as drugs and alcohol. Some of them even take their lives, just as many adults do.

Young people should be encouraged to resist perceived weaknesses or feelings of inadequacy. Individuals often seek relief from negative self- perceptions. One method of countering negative perceptions is to encourage youthful individuals, especially, to internalize what their Creator has proclaimed about them. From a biblical perspective, every human created has a destiny, a purpose upon which their fulfillment rests. They can resolve that it is the responsibility of the Creator to convey the purpose as well as provide the means to its achievement.

The primary responsibility of the creature is obedience, the only appropriate response. Any alternative concept of human existence places the responsibility of purpose, fulfillment and prevision on the creature itself. This would be a peculiar concept advocating each person created himself. The former thought leads one to accept that God is able to predetermine what is needed to fulfill each mission for each of His creations.

As a moral agent, God allows human beings to exercise reasoning, choice and other examples of independence. Nevertheless, He desires our relationship with Him to sustain us with positive representations in the world reflecting His goodness, *"You fill me with joy in Your presence"* -Psalm 16:11.

In our youthful experiences, the concept of created potential and created purpose provoke believers to test the validity of Romans 8:28 *"And we know that in all things God works for the good of those who love Him, who have been called according to his purpose"*. Romans 8:29, *"For those God foreknew He also predestined to be conformed to the image of His Son"*. A debate focused on predestination is not the purpose of this discussion. May it suffice to offer that a Creator has initiated purpose for His creation, man included. Logic presupposes the ability to create and the ability to sustain what has been created. The creature (man) is not expected to sustain himself. Rather, as long as the creature is engaged in its preordained purpose, his provision, protection (if needed) and fulfillment must depend on the Creator. The Creator is the only One who has all of the answers to all of the questions.

Created potential does not guarantee success or fulfillment. Potential in any form indicates just that, potential, that which is possible and what can be. God does not impose His will upon man at all times. However, He does communicate at a level of intelligence, leaving the free agency of man to operate in most of his own decisions. It appears that, at the point of a person's willful disobedience, God is not obligated to support the potential or purpose which has been instilled in an individual. Of course God's characteristic graciousness and mercy may supersede justifiable consequences within a person's life. I include the term "justifiable consequences" because God's character of justice provokes Him to forewarn individuals of the potential consequences of their decision.

Dr. Charles Stanley indicates that God created human beings with fellowship in mind. If that is accurate, every action or decision of the individual should have a goal, greater intimacy with God. It is with this mindset that created potential manifests itself into created purpose. Potential is meaningful only when it is activated. It has to be released and applied to an interaction of life. Potential energy has to become active in order to accomplish purpose.

Bishop Neil Ellis of Mt. Tabor Baptist Church in Nassau, Bahamas described the human potential and his connection with God. In Genesis 1:1, *"In the beginning God created the heavens and earth"*. Dr. Ellis reminds us that in Genesis 1:26,..."*Then God said, let us make mankind in our own image, in our likeness"*, then in Gen 1:27, *"God created mankind in His own image, in the image of God He created them"*. Dr. Ellis's point is that the Bible introduces a God who is creating marvelous entities who have no prior existence. Therefore, if God is a creative and important aspect of character of those made in His image and in His likeness, they should manifest similar potential. We should be creators, not necessarily creators of the same products but creators just the same.

Our youth should embrace the idea that God waits for the freedom to bless us (Dr. Charles Stanley). God is omnipotent. But He will not violate His own principles. He draws us to Himself so that we can experience His love and forgiveness. He asks for our willingness so that He can give us the best blessings He has to offer. It is this willingness which is a bridge between potential, purpose and accomplishment. It can also become the wall which blocks purpose, potential and achievement.

According to Anne Graham Lotz, she experienced many trials in the previous years, including her parents' serious illnesses and her son's battle with cancer. She shared with an interviewer that she finally came to the point where all she wanted was Jesus. "Just give me Jesus," she declared. Mrs. Lotz realized that if she had a personal, intimate relationship with the Creator of the universe, whatever problems she faced, He would face them with her. He would bring resolution and peace to her life.

The cry of Anne Graham Lotz must be the cry of every human being. We are indeed all created equally; equal in purpose or value. A toe sustains as much value as a hand; equal potential, designed to contribute to efficiency and productivity of the entire human body. The divine connection serves to highlight the divine relationship needed to fulfill each person's destiny. Value must not be measured in dollars, cents or precious stones; value will be measured in view of eternity and obedience to the Creator.

The concept that identity with an omnipotent creator who designs with purpose and potential applies to the existence of every human being. Purposes and potential of men and women exist at levels superior to other creatures on earth. Human creation is set apart from any other creation. Aside from other attributes, man/woman, is/are the only being/beings whose primary purpose for existence is to fellowship with the Creator.

From the previous perspective, the idea of one individual, or one created race being created superior to another is irrational, if not ludicrous. Creation is arbitrary to the Creator, not the option of the creature. To create one race of human beings superior to another serves no Godly purpose, no purpose for fellowship. A poorly educated farmer living in Ecuador can serve his purpose or fellowship, as well as, or perhaps more effectively than an Ivy League graduate. The farmer may better achieve his destiny since he may have less material distractions from his divine purpose. The more formally educated may divert energy to develop and debate sophisticated ideologies. He may even develop medical or social achievements that benefit the human race. If so, that person should be applauded for his accomplishments. However, does that achievement make him superior to the one who communes with the Creator and achieves peace, joy and contentment throughout a long life? Is either creation greater than the other or merely different? "Heaven forbid!", Apostle Paul exclaims frequently when the response to a question is negative. Degrees of temporal achievements do not reflect greater ability or significance. Frequently, they actually reflect earthly choices and opportunities. Good, better, best are relative descriptions influenced by one's point of view, biases or value system.

Early in life, young people around the world could benefit from adopting the philosophy conveyed by Job 10:12, *"You gave me life and showed me kindness and in your providence, watched over my spirit"*. The interpretation is *"...God sustains everyone, even when we cannot see His hand in our situations"*. The young might understand that all individuals are truly equal, in terms of their origin, value and source of existence. Where they are born or when they were born has little relevance if God has established the purpose for their existence. In Samuel 9:21, Saul thought of himself as small but God loves to use the weak things of the world to shame the strong. That way, they are assured that the victories we enjoy are by His hand and not our own (2 Cor.12:9-10), Charles F. Stanley Life Principles Bible.

Regardless of how superior one perceives himself or envisions his status, ethnicity or race, the truth is, "Before the mountains were born or brought forth, the whole world…You are God (Psalms 90:2)". Ultimately, God turns people back to dust (Psalms 90:3) after their earthly existence has expired.

In 1988, Dr. Ken Magid collaborated with Carole A. McKelvey to compose a book, *High Risk: Children Without a Conscience*. Dr. Magid was a renowned expert on theory techniques, addressing major issues of attachment theory, diagnosis of high risk children, educational options, treatment and follow-up. An excerpt from the book:

America, land of the free or breeding ground for psychopaths. Hundreds of thousands of individuals filled with hatred populate this country. They are people without a conscience, and they hurt, sometimes kill, without remorse. They are psychopaths and possess a poisonous mix of traits. They are arrogant, shameless, immoral, antisocial, superficial, charming, callous, irresponsible, irreverent, cunning, self-assured. They are found in jails and mental institutions but they can also be found in boardrooms or politics in any number of respected professions. (pp. 1-2)

According to unconfirmed reports, George Bernard Shaw, the famous Irish playwright uttered the following, "Life is a flame that is always burning itself out, but it catches fire again, every time a child is born". This hopeful precept suggests that behaviors and beliefs are successive with each generation. Practices are learned and those which manifest preternatural inclinations that are corrupt emanate from a corrupt spirit. This undesirable behavior persists if not corrected by training or highly significant emotional events. The ultimate cure, if there is one, to altering the pervasive psychological behavior is by converting the life script of a child, rather than investing in the synthetic chemicals and the adult therapeutics. Benjamin Franklin is credited with proclaiming, "Sin is not hurtful because it is forbidden, but it is forbidden because it is hurtful."

I accept there is a curative agent for sin, especially behavior which harms people. Many people believe that administering the death penalty consistently and generously would reduce the act of murder. Years of statistics fail to support that position. It appears that capital punishment is merely a reactionary step. It fails to assist the victim or the perpetrator. There is minimal solace provided to the loved ones of the victim. My first hand experience in this regard affirms how little healing is generated as a result of revenge killing. I advocate proactive decision making to address the critical behavior and consequences. Capital punishment is reactionary decision making at its highest level.

Several notable references indicate that the source of human life is the creator, God. Some people dismiss this concept as simplistic and illogical. For clarity, this writing is directed toward individuals who consider themselves believers. Those who abide by the creation standard. These are the called out ones. The ones in 2 Chronicles 7:14... *"If my people, who are called by my name, shall humble themselves, and pray, and seek my face and turn from their wicked ways, then will I hear from heaven, and will forgive their sin, and heal their land".* The people, must possess a different perspective about humanity and matters pertaining to humanity. Job 10:8 declares *"Your hands shaped and made me...and remember that you molded me like clay"*, Finally, Job 10:11.. *"Did you not clothe me with skin and flesh and knit me together with bones and sinews?"*.

To me, the logical action when my wife's Jaguar has mechanical trouble is to contact a mechanic trained in serving Jaguars. I could also contact someone who has built a Jaguar. These specialists may be more expensive than a general mechanic, yet, I am assured of fewer problems in the future. It belongs to my wife, but I like it too. So, when I have a chance to drive it, I want it to run well. It is a good quality automobile and it costs us something. I help her take care of it because we expect it to last. It runs well so we may not invest in another second vehicle for a long, long time.

Human lives are valuable as well. Our youth are valuable and vulnerable. So, adults need to invest more time, more energy and sometimes more resources to make sure the youth turn out well, not perfect. Not even our Jaguar is perfect. Aside from the occasional human issues, adults can refer to the Creator and His guide for helping the young "turn out right". There are always expectations and problems beyond human limitations, but we can increase the odds to favor our youth.

One way is to introduce them to their Creator at an early age, and encourage them to get to know him well. He already knows them very well. Encourage them to study his word and search out the plan the Creator had for their lives. Help them understand the privilege of allowing him to guide their decisions and forgive and repair their mistakes.

In Daniel chapter one, Daniel and his associates refrain from consuming foods that perhaps cause them long-term health problems. Bishop T.D. Jakes, out of Texas, admonishes parents to teach their children to train their appetites. Parents must teach their children to draw the line to resist many things that fuel their appetites. This restraint helps the children to grow and maintain their divine connection to their Creator. The ability to accept the existence of divine connection can help youth discover their divine purpose. This discussion provokes a necessary debate among youth and the adults who touch their lives. It challenges the proclivity toward participation in unprovoked violence, physical abuse and educational failure.

In chapter 5, considerable time addresses the disproportionate number of African-American children and other groups of color channeled into public school special education programs in America. I challenge the reliability of statistics which justify this ratio. I believe there are biblical implications which decry the acceptance or normalcy of these scenarios.

A prominent idea of this book is the proposal that God... The Creator has designed each individual, even prior to birth, capable of fulfilling his/her purpose in the world (Jeremiah 1:6). Adults have the responsibility of assisting young people in discovering purpose, talents and gifts for the journey they have been fitted for. Adults are needed to assist the youth in discovering what God has designed for them. Unfortunately, preconceived notions about certain children disregards their value and capability. In respect of their divine nature or purpose, this bias submerges them into low performing ability groups or special education tracts. Modifications in some of these programs are frequently derived from erroneous diagnoses. Too often it has been my observation. The decision to address the student's difficulty includes the application of medicine. These decisions derive from the well meaning clinician in concert with frustrated teachers and parents seeking relief from a challenging situation in the classroom.

It is critical that more time, objectively, and spirituality be employed when determining action which will affect a child's life. This book will probably experience very limited readership. Its premise, as mentioned, is based on the truth that each person possesses the entities of mind, soul, spirit and body. It also presupposes that the spirit and mind are areas which allow more interaction of ideas. This position also correlates with the supposition that those two areas demonstrate how thinking and behavior of our youth are manifested.

In the beginning, God created the heavens and the earth (Genesis 1:1). If we are going to be productive, we should commence at the beginning. If we cannot agree on the mitral concept, we are not able to proceed further. Then, in Genesis 1:27, *"God created mankind in His own image, in the image of God, He created them"*. I often share with participants in Christian leadership workshops that if we cannot agree on the inerrant truth of the scriptures, we cannot agree on any other spiritual matter. In which case, we should just give our opinions about sports or discuss politics. We will conclude at the same points: infinite opinions, there has to be a standard of truth, a termination by which we can establish the veracity of everything else. In instances where interpretations can vary, because the Bible is not explicit, we respect reasonable discourse and proceed with the information which does not require interpretation. Honor thy mother and father, honor the Lord thy God, do not steal. Those commandments are pretty clear; there are many others. I readily admit that there is antiquated phraseology, unfamiliar cultural communications and unique poetic discourse which lend themselves to broad interpretation and scholarly debate. These debates can serve useful purposes in academic discussions, however, for the purposes of providing veritable support.

To help today's youth experience fulfilling lives the instructions must be clear. Motives must be pure and the path proven. For example, terms such as "productive" or "fulfilling" are not necessarily synonymous in a secular world with the wealthy and popular. Unfortunately, some adults and young people adopt the idea that material wealth and happiness are equal. One day, they will discover that their large bank account fails to ease their emotional pain, and their designer clothes and fashionable car is impotent at alleviating a broken heart, despair, mental anguish or emptiness. Some people discover too late that no assortment of ingested substances can provide a solution for years of regret and bad decisions.

On the contrary, a productive and fulfilling life reflects life experiences, which align with one's innate capacity: activity which offers satisfaction, peace of mind and spirit, sufficiency for material needs, creativity for the soul and contentment that he has achieved meaningful purpose with service to others and one's Creator. Young people should be reminded continually that God created them in His own image, His own reflection. When other people see them, they are viewing representations of God. What is God like? In a 365- day study titled, _Sparkling Gems_, it includes one lesson, "It's Time to Act Like God". At first viewing, the title sounds blasphemous. No one should act like God, we protest! Nevertheless, how often have sons been reminded, "you act like your father" or daughters hear, "You sound and look like your mother"? We accept those kinds of expressions as commendable, especially if the parents possess laudable qualities. The announcement about the similarity frequently stimulates feelings of pride in the children who resemble their parents. Parents may receive enjoyment if they are informed how much their child behaves as they do. The joy may expand when a mechanic hears that his son or daughter demonstrates his mechanical interest or a mother who is informed how much her child resembles her style and aptitude for the piano may beam with delight. Both children and parents can experience pleasure when these characteristics are recognized and echoed. Frankly, if a strong bond exists between the parent and the child, the latter frequently strives to magnify the kinship with the parent.

Coming from the Southern United States under the astute eye of a shrewd aunt, my cousin and I were regularly admonished as we departed for some social event: "Remember who you are; don't do anything to embarrass me! The admonishment, perhaps, occasionally contributed to a hypersensitive consciousness of right and wrong. As I matured into adulthood, that sensitivity probably morphed into judgmental self-righteousness toward the behavior of others. This attitude occurred due to my failure to equate my aunt's love with her desire to protect me from harm. In retrospect, I understand the depth of her concern. I grew to venture into the world motivated by my appreciation. I endeavored to make sure any feedback she received about me was pleasing to her ears. I was pleased to be identified as Tang's boy. The positive tone stimulated gratification. Over time, other people's views or whether those opinions reached my aunt ceased to be important. My fulfillment was sustained in the knowledge that I had represented her well. At that stage of our relationship, her trust had grown. The reminders about my behavior ceased. The trust was actually mutual. For me, I stopped considering whether she could see me or hear anything about my behavior. The fact that she trusted me and loved me escalated my love and respect for her. It was like I loved her because she first loved me (1 John 4:19). My motivation to please her drove me to increase my efforts in the classroom as well as in the cotton field.

This represents the life challenge adults must help our youth recognize and mimic. They need to accept that God created them. He must be recognized as their beginning and that He loved them before they were aware of themselves. Jeremiah 10:23 declares, *"Lord, I know that people's lives are not for them to direct their steps"*. Instead, God made us to be dependent on Him for guidance and counsel. Dr. Charles Stanley reminds us that, "We commit our lives to God, not only for salvation, but for what we need and where we go every moment of our lives". All things have been created through Him and for Him (Colossians 1:15-16).

The prophet, Jeremiah, assures us that, *"Blessed is the one who trusts in the Lord, whose confidence is in Him. They will be like a tree planted by the water that sends out its roots by the stream"*. In Jeremiah: God attests... before He *"formed you in the womb"* He knew each one of us. He further confirms,..." *before you (we) were born, He set us apart"*. He appointed us for a specific purpose. In Jeremiah's case, his mission was to be a prophet.

In David's case, it was to be king of Israel. Samson's call was to use Godly superhuman strength to save His people from the Philistines and Moses was to lead God's people out of slavery from Egyptian rule. The illustrations are plentiful but they are not necessarily exceptional. Each individual revealed flaws and proclivity to sin. This is a truth which young people can benefit from. God assigns us a purpose by which to glorify Him even while we are still in the womb. Even though He has prepared the plan of salvation for our sins, He knows that the curse of the sinful nature abides on and in us. This knowledge does not nullify His plan for us. Instead, young people must learn that the plan God has for their lives supersedes the wrongful actions they may succumb to. If they will trust Him, He can solve the sinful nature so that they can grasp their identity as a created being in the hands of a loving God. That realization introduces them to their created potential.

Young people must confront a critical question. It is one of the defining questions of their existence as a human being. Am I created by God? That question is imperative. The answer to the question is equally urgent. If the answer is affirmative, a flood of ideas and realizations follow which impact attitudes and philosophies toward life. This attitude frames one's concepts about self, others, purpose on earth and value system. An affirmative response also helps youth finalize how to invest one's time, energy and effort. If a young person believes that a power greater than himself or herself brought them into existence, the concept of conferring with that supreme being for knowledge is not unreasonable. The fact that a guidebook (Bible) exists, as well as opportunities to confer with an omniscient being (Holy Spirit) who wants to help, can reduce an exceptional amount of stress in adolescents or their life.

Acceptance of creation minimizes time wasted searching for purpose. Subsequent frustration and disappointment can be reduced. One spiritual leader expressed, we learn quickly that our achievements in life may be affected by feelings of inability, inadequacy or inferiority. Jeremiah 1:6 complains to God, *"If I do not know how to speak, I am too young"*. However, in Jeremiah 1:8, God responds, *"Do not be afraid of them; for I am with you and will rescue you"*. Of course, Jeremiah heard God speaking to him. Some people might attest, "If I heard God speaking to me, I would refrain from fear". That appears reasonable yet there are instances recorded in The Bible where God's audible voice was ignored by the person who heard it. More significantly is the existence of a God capable of creating human beings' talent, creativity and incredible intelligence.

From a Judea-Christian perspective, several alternative theories about creation are quite preposterous. For example, the theory of spontaneous organic existence appeared haphazard. According to that concept, undetermined beings appeared possessing no ordained purpose and no guiding principles. This concept can be confusing, even stressful for young people who are already struggling with emotions and life issues such as their future, family or death of loved ones. Settling the question of one's existence, deriving from and for a specific purpose introduces stability. It presents the probability that an individual is created for a specific purpose and created potential. Clarity and healthy possibilities can blossom. Meaningful direction seems possible. Within such a culture, internal motivation can itself evolve, perpetuating individuals toward growth and completeness. Youngsters can be propelled to fulfill goals for their lives. The goals would be characterized by meaningful activity producing healthy self-satisfaction in the areas of emotional, psychological and spiritual health.

DIVINE CONNECTION

Divine Connection exposes that human beings are created for the purpose of fellowshipping with God, their Creator. Divine Connection further advocates that by right of creatorship, God can exercise total authority over the human race. This ultimate authority extends beyond their use of time on earth or how their talents are utilized along with the consideration of the gifts and resources He provides. Reciprocal relationship would anticipate that humans seek guidance for how the Creator desires His resources to be used. Psalms 91:15 illustrates how humans, via prayer, connect our needs with God's supply. We bring our emptiness to God's bountiful love and provisions and ask Him to satisfy our needs.

Young people can learn that their deficits are no match for God's abundance. Subsequently, He assumes full responsibility for needs when we obey Him (Philippians 4:19), "...and God will meet all our needs according to the riches of His glory in Christ Jesus". I have already discussed Dr. Magid's research involving *Children Without a Conscience*. One of his conclusions was that there is no cure for adult pathology of psychopathic behavior. I propose that acceptance of Divine Connection is indeed the only remedy for adults and the cure for High Risk children. I will elaborate. In chapter 6 of Dr. Magid's book, there is discussion of <u>Childhood Symptoms: A Warning of Things to Come</u>. The list of symptoms will sound familiar to those in the psychology field and perhaps parents or teachers in many of the nation's schools. The list is lengthy but far from exhaustive:

1) Lack of ability to give and receive affection
2) Self-destructive behavior
3) Cruelty to others or to pets
4) Phoniness
5) Stealing, hoarding and gorging
6) Speech pathology
7) Extreme control problems
8) Lack of long term childhood friends
9) The parents seem unreasonably angry
10) Abnormalities in eye contact
11) Preoccupation with blood, fire and gore
12) Superficial attractiveness and friendliness with strangers
13) Learning disorders
14) Crazy lying

(Cline, 1974)

Dr. Magid extracted the list of symptoms from compilations of Cornell Watkins and professor Walt Schreibman of the Youth Behavior Program. Mr. Watkins and Mr. Schreibman obtained feedback from files shared by Dr. Forster Cline. Dr. Cline was a leading authority on unattached children whom he treated over 20 years. The list of symptoms as well as some of the research is dated. Dr. Cline granted access to his files in 1979. Psychological research itself has advanced considerably since that time, however, professional educators in some of our urban and suburban public schools recognize many of these symptoms. They are included in the broad criteria utilized to determine a student's need for psychological services in a special education program. Several of these symptoms, when identified, lead to many students being separated from the "regular" school education program; they often are classified as disruptive, incorrigible, or dangerous to themselves or others.

Educators and mental health professionals, along with parents and guardians can help all students succeed. As mentioned earlier, there are human limitations in any circumstances that may require supernatural assistance. Making a solitary effort to assist students who demonstrate numerous psychological symptoms is a yeoman's task. Interacting successfully with adults exhibiting similar behaviors can prove dangerous or hopeless.

Clearly, there is little or nothing illustrated in the adverse symptoms previously listed that suggests positive divine nature. The following is a list of behaviors which are the goal of Divine Connection:

1) Isaiah 26:3 *"...You will keep in perfect peace those whose minds are steadfast, because they trust in You (God)"*.

2) Isaiah 40:30-31, *"He gives strength to the weary and increases the power of the weak. Even when youths grow tired and weary, and young men stumble and fall; but those who hope in the Lord will renew their strength. They will soar on wings like eagles; they will run and not grow weary, they will walk and not faint"*.

3) Isaiah 41:10, *"..so do not fear for I am with you, do not be dismayed, for I am your God. I will strengthen you and help you ...I will uphold you with my righteous right hand"*.

4) Isaiah 43, *"Do not fear, for I am with you"*.

5) Isaiah 49:13, *"shout for joy, boast into song, for the Lord comforts His people and will have compassion"*.

6) Colossians 2:6-7, *"Continue to live your lives in Him, rooted and built up in Him, strengthened as you were taught and overflowing with thankfulness"*.

7) Colossians 3:18-22, *"Submit yourselves as fitting in the Lord"*.

8) Colossians 3:19, *"..love and do not be harsh"*.

9) Colossians 3:20, *"..children, obey your parents..."*

10) Colossians 3:21, *"Fathers, do not embitter your children.."*

11) Colossians 3:23, *"Whatever you do, work at it with all your heart"*

12) Colossians 4:1. *"Provide what is right"*

These behaviors and attitudes are commendable. Many adults would enjoy interacting with youngsters who are doing right, polite, respectful, honest, dependable, obedient and pleasant. Unfortunately, such benevolent displays are rare among many young people we observe.

Even young people who have attended formal religious churches for significant time throughout their lives are difficult to distinguish judging from their contrary behavior outside of ecclesiastical environment. Some achieved perfect attendance in Sunday School, certificates in vacation bible school and day camp. Others performed moving solos in the junior choir at Easter and Christmas plays.

What happened? With the exposure to Christian activity, why is there not a consistent display of more favorable behavior among the teenagers as well as young adults of similar background. One pastor of a conservative Baptist church protested his exasperation, "We send our children to the church school for 12 years, then on graduation night they go out and get drunk!". What is the problem? Maybe the youth were only exposed to the church and its religious activity. They were immersed in the divine atmosphere, however, perhaps failed to experience a highly emotionally significant event for themselves. An emotional event needed to help them realize their identity or to accept the responsibility to their Creator, themselves, their ancestors and to posterity.

Church is not the only place where well rounded young people can be produced or cultivated. It certainly, we hope, is one of the preeminent institutions which can obtain such goals. I propose that churches or other religious institutions serious about contributing to the development of balanced young people re-examine their goals and beliefs for their young people. Let us commence with some observations various churches teach their young people about having a relationship with God. That concept is generally encased in the process called salvation.

YOUTH MUST REALIZE THEIR RESPONSIBILITY TO

1. Creatorship
2. Self
3. Ancestors
4. Posterity

The previous scripture references illustrate the importance of a relationship with Christ, the Son of God. What may be lacking is the understanding that each person has a divine responsibility. That responsibility translates into quarterly manifestations. We shall examine the four relationships.

Young people must realize their responsibility to their Creator. The question of creatorship is a forgone conclusion from this perspective. The question pending is what does that responsibility to the Creator look like?

At one point the Israelites were warned that if parents sinned, the children's teeth were set on edge. The concept was that children suffered for the sins of their parents. However, with the advent of Christ even, this principle changed. God does not punish children for their parent's sins. Of course it is possible for children to suffer consequences of parent's behavior, yet, those effects are coincidental rather than consequential (Dt. 24:16, Ezekiel 18:20). Nevertheless, parents must understand that they may, through their sins, inflict pervasive harm on their children, even influencing them to do evil. Parents must be conscientious to rear their children to love and respect God (Proverbs 22:6, Ephesians 6:4, Colossians 3:21). In Matthew 19:14, Jesus said, *"Let the little children come to me and do not hinder them, for the kingdom belongs to such as these"*.

These illustrations reflect the behavior parents can display to help their children exemplify their responsibility to their Creator. The parents perform in ways which demonstrate their allegiance or connection to their children. This allegiance guides them toward making decisions about their use of time and resources. It also contributes to their awareness of personal testimony.

Young people can exercise methods by which they demonstrate appreciation and allegiance to their Creator. Throughout the Bible, God describes the behavior that He expects from those whom He has created and gifted with talents and given responsibilities. In Genesis chapter 2, after God had created man and woman, He commanded the man, *"You are free to eat from any tree in the garden, but you must not eat from the Tree of Knowledge of Good and Evil"*. Earlier in Genesis 1:29, God said to Adam, *"Be fruitful and multiply (increase) in number; fill the earth and subdue it. Rule over the fish in the sea and the birds in the sky and over every living creature that moves on the ground"*.

It appears that some of the expectations God had for Adam and Eve were beyond their human capability to fulfill. They could not fly to subdue the birds in the air. They could not travel the expanse of the sea to subdue the sea creatures. However, in Genesis 2:19-20, God had provided a means for the man to adhere to his God given responsibilities,

> *"..Now the Lord God had formed out of the ground all the wild animals and all the birds in the sky. He brought them to man to see what he would name them; and whatever the man called each living creature, that was its name. So, the man gave names to all the livestock, the birds in the sky and all the wild animals"*.

God provided the means in Genesis 2 so that Adam could carry out what he had been instructed to do in Genesis chapter 1. That is amazing! This example could encourage young people. Adam demonstrated obedience by naming the animals, etc. That was his responsibility, to obey God's command. He did not need to gather tools and weapons, like a great hunter tramping in the jungle like a safari.

All Adam did was wait for God to bring all of the animals to him. Considering the monumental task many Bible scholars assume that God also provided Adam and Eve with exceptional intelligence and creativity. Even though Adam and Eve spoiled a good thing in chapter 3 of Genesis, chapters 1 & 2 illustrate how much God can do through us if we strive to represent Him through obedience. Their responsibility was to obey, God took care of the rest.

There are other examples of mankind carrying out the responsibilities given by God. If Noah had not represented God through obedience, no humans or animals would have survived the flood. It is a fact that if one person does accept a responsibility, God can find or prepare someone else to carry out the task. As a Creator, He has the capacity to enable anyone for His purpose. However, young people need to consider that as Jeremiah understood, "God, You knew me before I was formed in my mother's womb". Prior to being born into this world, God predetermined where we needed to be in this world; what region, country, state, family, etc. Young people can consider that He knew what events needed to be ordained for their existence to develop the personality that He desired for them.

We must remind young people that the perfect order where God created and man obeyed changed, after the sin of Adam in the Garden of Eden. The road from birth to obedience and blessing has gotten much more difficult and often dusty. It has become confusing sometimes to reason how or why God would allow certain events into our lives, or into the lives of others. In the corrupt human mind, it is a challenge to accept certain instances as predetermined. Some events appear brutal and heartless. Even so, young people can be assured that their responsibility is to strive to obey God's direction in every way they understand. God promises that He accepts responsibility for the consequences, *"And we know that all things work together for those who love Him and who are called according to His purpose (Romans 8:28)"*.

In this world of disappointments, it may be difficult for young people to imagine an all-powerful God who instills specific skills into one individual for a special purpose. Let us consider other examples. First, note this disclaimer: since God is God, there is no reason that He cannot provide multiple talents to one individual while providing less to another. There is no implication that the person with several talents is more significant than the person with one ability. The responsibility individuals have is to obey God based on one's understanding of God's desire. That responsibility cannot be consummated unless each person acquires accurate information. Reliable information can be obtained by praying and listening to God, reading God's word regularly, talking to and listening to mature believers who pray themselves and studying God's word. Even if an individual tries his best, very likely, mistakes will occur; he may miss the mark regarding what God desires him to do. Nevertheless, God's promise is reliable. Jeremiah 33:3 says *"Call unto me and I will show you great and mighty things that you do not know"*.

Young people have a responsibility to obey their Creator, obey and respect their parents and respect God's creation (other people, resources, self and other creatures). God punished the Israelites because they failed to properly take care of the land He had provided and when they failed to take care of His House of Worship (Jeremiah 7:10-14).

God was even angry when His children just failed to listen. Ezekiel chapter 2 says, *"Son of man (Ezekiel), I am sending you to the Israelites, to a rebellious nation that has rebelled against Me; they and their ancestors have been in revolt against me; the people to whom I am sending you are obstinate and stubborn"*.

The preceding examples offer a picture of what responsibility to God entails. The Creator expects by right of his creatorship, for His creatures to respond to and represent Him on the earth that He created. Being responsible to one's Creator is a reasonable expectation. However, that level of responsibility extends further. God identifies His human creation as extremely valuable, made in His image (Gen. 1:26-27). With the establishment of personhood, God laid out the superior plans and endeavors that He envisioned for men and women. He clearly outlined the responsibility each person has to himself or herself. Genesis 1:26 says God blessed them and said to them,

"Be fruitful and multiply (increase in number). Fill the earth and subdue it. Rule over the fish in the sea, and the birds in the sky and over every living creature that moves on the ground". Genesis 1:29 continues,

"Then God said, I give you every seed-bearing plant on the face of the whole earth and every tree that has fruit with seed in it. They will be your food. To all the beasts of the earth, and all the birds in the sky, and all the creatures that move along the ground...everything that has the breath of life in it".

Within these verses, God has clearly articulated commands. However, these commands if carried out do not benefit God. These directions are for the benefit of mankind. Young people must learn that, based on the Word of God, they have a responsibility to themselves. God has directed, "I have given you everything you need for food, for fulfillment, for recreation, etc". You have been made in My image. Do something meaningful with your time, your talents, your life. We should remind our youth that their talents are special, whatever they are, but they should be used to improve something in our time on this earth. God seems to assert, "I have given you everything you need, now do something worthwhile with it". We have seen throughout the Bible where God raises up people who have special talents and gifts to accomplish incredible tasks. Since creation, God never relinquished His control over the destiny of human beings. Jeremiah 1:3, *"Before I formed you in the womb, I knew you. Before you were born, I set you apart. I appointed you as a prophet to the nations".* Then in Jeremiah 29:11, He reminds Jeremiah, *"For I know the plans I have for you, plans to prosper you and not harm you, plans to give you hope and a future".* God wants His human creations to maintain an intimate relationship with Him. Jeremiah 29:12, *"Then you will call on Me and pray to Me and I will listen to you".*

Our responsibility to ourselves is to maximize our talents to glorify God to benefit others and the world. God loves us and He has invested Himself in us. He has given Himself completely to us and we are obligated to devote ourselves to Him and His purpose (Charles Stanley, "Life Lessons"). All too frequently, young people voice questions and frustrations about not knowing what to do with their lives. Various aptitude tests have been developed to provide insight into the strengths of individuals. These assessments can be useful, especially when exploring levels of technical potential, when exploring careers. However, there are examples listed in the Bible where God identifies individuals or groups that He has given the talented skills for that purpose. We will review some of them. There is a consideration young people should ponder. God may not provide directions and assign talents for a career; instead, He may have a greater purpose. He will provide directions for your life. He will structure your life experiences to support and help you reach your destiny.

In 1 Chronicles 15, David has made preparations return to the ark of God to Jerusalem. Upon informing the Israelites of his plans, He reminded them, *"No one but the Levites may carry the ark of God because the Lord chose them to carry the ark...and to minister before Him forever"*. David reminds the Israelites that God was angry with them before because His directions had not been followed. This time, *"...and the Levites consecrated themselves in order to bring up the Ark of the Lord... and the Levites carried the ark of God on poles on their shoulders, as Moses had commanded in accordance with the Word of the Lord"*. As part of the ceremony, David directed the Levites to appoint their fellow Levites as musicians to make music with musical instruments such as the lyre, harps and cymbals. These directions had been prescribed by God. He specified the instruments and the people who were to provide the music. In verse 19 of chapter 15, the guidelines are more specific: the musicians Herman, Asaph and Ethan were to sound the bronze cymbals. Jehiel, Unni and Eliab, Marseial and Benaiah were to play the lyres according to the alamo (musical term). Mattithich, Elipheleu, Mikneia, Obed-Edom, Jiel and Azaziah were to play the harps, according to Sheminith (musical term). Kenaniah, the head Levite, was in charge of the singing; that was his responsibility because he was skillful at it. Verse 23 says Berekiah and Elkanah were to be door keepers for the ark. Shebaniah, Joshaphat, Nethanel, Amasal, Zechariah, Benaiah and Eliezeith, the priest, were to blow trumpets before the ark of God. Obed-Edom and

Jehiah were also to be doorkeepers for the ark. Verse 27 indicates, *"and Kenaniah was in charge of the singing of the choirs"*.

It is fascinating how detailed the directions are regarding which Levites performed in this important musical procession. It is possible that David or an assistant possessed foreknowledge of the talents possessed by certain individuals. Perhaps, David was skilled in delegating responsibility to individuals based on their interests and gifts. Both of these scenarios are probable. Nevertheless, based on David's earlier reference, God was angry earlier about the mishandling of the ark of God.

We can infer that David would have received directions from God so that additional mistakes could be avoided. After all, God was the one who would know which individuals were especially qualified for certain tasks. He would know because He had provided the skills that would honor Him.

Our young people must learn that, though they may have multiple talents and interests, as many people do, God has provided them all to be used for purposes that He has predetermined. When we obey by using our God given talents for His purposes, He is not only glorified and pleased, but our efforts at obedience motivate Him to bless us in more ways than we can predict. Obedience to His will frees us from the need to carry burdens of frustration and anxiety about "what am I going to do with my life?". God had those answers before He placed us in this world. The frustration persists or increases when we fail to trust that there is a God who cares for us and wants the best for us. He is the same God who offers, *"Cast your cares on Me because I care for you"*. The God who promises, *"Call unto Me and I will answer you (James 33:3)"*. He even makes greater promises, no matter what you may experience, remember to *"Seek ye first the kingdom of God and His righteousness and all other things will be added to you (Matthew 6:33)"*. These scriptures do not convey earthly bliss because we place our trust in God that we would have no challenges or trouble. That is false. The first guarantee is that if we allow Him to guide us into the areas He has planned for us, He accepts responsibility for all of the consequences. That alone can stimulate tremendous relief in a world plagued by uncertainty. The holy scriptures also do not declare that you will not have to contest for possession of what God has ordained for you. There are evil forces, often working through people and circumstances, which will make an effort to discourage you from your God given purpose. When these situations occur, our responsibility is to strive to get closer to God, by spending more time with him in prayer and study of His word. If He has ordained you for a purpose here on earth and provided you with the gifts, talents and desire to achieve that purpose, the only thing evil people can do is discourage you. They can maybe even make things inconvenient, hoping that you give up on your goals or God's purpose. They cannot defeat God's purpose. When these difficult times come in your life, check what God told Joshua, *"Be strong and of good courage"*. The phrase, "good courage", is an unusual description. It is the only place in The Bible where it is used. It appears that God, in His onescienous (all knowing), foresees the kind of difficulty Joshua is going to face in his future as the leader of Israel. Yet, in a similar certainty associated with His sovereignty and power, he reminds Joshua," Do not be afraid; do not be discouraged," because I will be you every step of the way. No one will be able to stand up against you. They may resist you but they will not be able to stop you from achieving what God has created you for. We must trust that God is all powerful and the Creator of Heaven and Earth. In 1 Chronicles, David reminds the people how God protected His people from one enemy after another. He allowed no one to oppress them...for their sake He rebuked kings. In 1 Chronicles 16:25, *"For great is the Lord and most worthy of praise, He is to be feared above all gods. For all the gods of the nations are idols but the Lord made the heavens ...strength and joy are in His dwelling place"*.

In 1 Chronicles, we see David expand the list of assignments for people to participate in the worship before the ark of the covenant. He left Asaph and his associates before the ark...to minister regularly according to each day's requirements. He also left Obed-Edom and his sixty eight associates to minister with them. Obed-Edom and Hosah were gatekeepers, with them were Herman and Jeduthun and the rest of the chosen and designated by name to give thanks to the Lord. He and Jeduthun were responsible for the sounding of the trumpets.

David had been faithful to his God given task as King of Israel. He wanted to demonstrate his love for God. He decided to build a permanent temple for the ark of God. Until that time the ark, like the Israelites, had travelled from place to place. David's desire was appreciated by God. God, however, had a different plan. In 1 Chronicles 17, He told David, *"When your days are over and you go to be with your ancestors, I will raise up your offspring to succeed you. He is the one who will build a house for Me. I will set him over My house and My kingdom forever".* Later in chapter 17, David concedes to God's plan, *"and now Lord, let the promise You have made concerning Your servant and his house be established forever, do as You promised". "Now You have been pleased to bless the house of Your servant, that it may continue forever in Your sight. For you, Lord, have blessed it and it will be blessed forever".*

These acclamations of God reveal David's confidence in God's faithfulness and His ability to carry out, in the future, exactly what He says. It is significant how God is the only person who can make promises concerning future events. He is also the only one who can prepare people and resources that are guaranteed to carry out His plans in the distant future. To help David carry out his assignment, several people were identified. They possessed the necessary skills so that God's plans for David's life and reign were carried out. Joab, son of Zeruiah, was over the army. Jehosaphat, son of Ahilud was a recorder. Zadok, son of Ahitub and Ahimlek, son of Abiathar, were priests. Shausha was secretary; Benaiah, son of Jehoia, was over the Kerethites and Pelethites..David's sons were chief officials at the king's side.

Even though David was not going to build the temple for the ark of God, God gave him the opportunity to acquire all of the materials needed to complete the structure after his son, Solomon, became king. God also identified the craftsman and other skilled workers who would be available to complete the project. Before his death, David advised his son, Solomon,

> *"Now my son, the Lord be with you and may you have success and build the house of the Lord your God. May the Lord give you discretion and understanding when He puts you in command over Israel, so that you may keep the law of the Lord your God. Then, you will have success if you are careful to observe the decrees and laws that the Lord gave Moses. Be*

strong and courageous, do not be afraid or discouraged". 1
Chronicles 22:15, *"You have many workers, stone cutters,
masons, carpenters as well as those skilled in every kind of
work in gold and silver, bronze and iron. Now begin the
work, and the Lord be with you".*

The objective in this section of the book is to persuade young people
that there really is someone greater than anyone or anything, who cares
deeply for them. Young people can trust that they have been created for
a purpose. They are not in this world by accident. Perhaps, no one else
expected you to be born, but it was not a surprise or disappointment
to God. He wants our young people to understand that He has a plan
for their lives; a plan to help them and not to hurt or destroy them. He
encourages all young people to understand that He knows what their
heart desires. He has a healthy, safe method to show how to satisfy your
heart and help you to utilize all of the potential He has instilled in you.
To see this, you have to stand still long enough to get to know Him
and listen to Him. When you hurt, He hurts. He really wants what is
best for you. He can protect you; He can rescue you. He wants you to
have faith in Him. No one can understand you better than He does.
He created you, He knows exactly how to guide you when you need to
make important decisions. He knows your thoughts before they form
in your mind. You ask, why doesn't He stop me from doing some of
the unpleasant activities I have been in? Partly, He wants you to trust
Him enough to come to Him. Show some faith. He will then show
Himself to you. He will demonstrate how much He loves you through
the wonderful blessings He has for you. Young people, you are not alone.
Look closer at how much God did to help Solomon so that Solomon
could accomplish what he was created to do.

There is a contemporary gospel song which alludes to an event in
Genesis 22. The event is the relationship between God and Abraham.
At that point, Abraham is directed to sacrifice his son, Isaac. The line
from the song says, "You bring the fire, I'll bring the sacrifice". The
essence suggests that Abraham, in complete obedience to God, laid his
son on the altar as the sacrifice. God merely tested Abraham's obedience
and commitment and stopped Abraham before he struck his son.

Instead, God provided Himself a ram that had been stuck in the bushes. Abraham only had to slay the sacrifice that was supernaturally provided, using the fire he had brought. The example that was demonstrated in that passage is that, if we are obedient by doing what God directs us, God Himself will take care of everything else. When God gives us talents and gifts, we only need to use those gifts in a way which glorifies Him. What we cannot do, He will make up the difference so that the task He gave you can be completed. Your responsibility to God is to use what He has given you.

In chapter 23 of 1 Chronicles, King David is still advising his son, Solomon, the next king. I have directed all of the leaders of Israel to help you with the construction, protection and operation of the new temple. He says, *"Solomon, you have the support of over twenty thousand men to serve in different capacities. The descendants of Aaron will serve as priests, the Levites were to help Aaron's descendants in the service of the temple. According to David, some of the sons of Asaph, Heman and Jeduthun were responsible for prophesying that they would have harps, lyres and cymbal accompaniment"*. These men, under the supervision of the king, would work with their relatives because they were all trained and skilled in music for the Lord. All of these family members cast lots for their duties, the casting of lots was an accepted means of finding out God's will. There were other divisions, such as gatekeepers from the Korahite division. Other divisions included people who served as the treasurer and those who took care of every matter pertaining to the king. There were also leaders of the army division and king overseers. This included the royal store houses. There were storehouses in outlying districts, in towns, the villages and the watchtowers. Azmaveth was the son of Adiel. He was in charge of the royal store houses. Ezri, son of Kelub, was in charge of the workers who farmed the land. The following list identifies the persons and their responsibilities in the new kingdom, which was going to be headed by Solomon:

Shimei And Remathite- *in charge of vineyards*
Zabithe Shiphimile- *in charge of the produce of the vineyards for the wine vats*
Benal-Hanani The Gedrite- *in charge of the olive and sycamore fig trees in the western foothills*

Joah- in charge of supplies of olive oil
Shitral the Sharonite- in charge of herds grazing in Sharon
Shephat, son of Adial- in charge of herds in the valley
Obil, the Ishmaelite- in charge of the camels
Jahdiah, the Meronothite- in charge of the donkeys
Jaziz, the Hagrite- in charge of the flocks

The total list is more comprehensive than what space will allow in this writing. Suffice it to say that the tasks were specific and so were the specific skills to carry them out. To do their jobs well, certain skills were required. Some people were born with specific skills, other skills could be acquired by training. The important aspect of this conversation is that each individual possessed God's anointing to carry out His task. They were aware that they were in service to the king, king of Israel and king of the universe. They had the assurance that they were well suited and prepared for their assignments. Success requires obedience and commitment. David reminds his son,... *"Acknowledge the God of your father and serve Him with wholehearted devotion and with a willing mind. For the Lord searches every heart and understands every desire and every thought. If you seek Him, He will be fond of you; but if you forsake Him, He will reject you forever (1 Chronicles 28:9)".*

My singular purpose is to challenge young people to consider, quite seriously, their heritage and future, that perhaps they have been designed for a particular, significant purpose. They may have dreams of stardom and fame. There is nothing inherently inappropriate about exciting dreams. Someone may also imagine themselves affluent, with riches and other possessions. There is nothing wrong with wealth and material possessions. It becomes problematic if one person dedicates his life and effort to these ends, only to determine at life's ultimate end that the only thing left is emptiness and uncertainty. Dozens of celebrities take their own lives while still at the peak of popularity. Many males and females choose suicide over continuing to live among their riches and fame. Why? There are certainly various reasons. What is certain is that the popularity or the wealth failed to add value to their life. Stardom was an insufficient reason to remain in this world. Obviously, there must be some people who enjoy their fame and fortune. No one knows if they fulfilled their ultimate purpose. No one will know, before eternity kicks in, if they have lived successfully, but not purposefully. Life after death may not be rewarding. I propose to air on the side of what appears most logical. The idea that a being who possesses intelligence and unimaginable creativity created other exceptional creatures is quite reasonable to me. Yet, my goal is not to debate theories of evolution versus creation. My desire is to establish that the incredible skill and potential possessed by human beings have been produced by another similar, though superior possessor of such skill and power. *"Before I formed you in the womb, I knew you. Before you were born, I set you apart. I appointed you as a prophet (Jeremiah 1:5)"*. Unlike Jeremiah, everyone has not been created to be a prophet. Nevertheless, just like Jeremiah, every human being has been created to serve a purpose. Then God said, *"Let us make mankind in Our image (Genesis 1:26)"*.

In order to structure one's life around this idea, it is inevitable for one to accept that The Bible is indeed true. It was spoken by God to man who recorded Elohim's words. The Bible confirms the creation of human beings for divine purpose. For all practical purposes the veracity of the Bible must be accepted on this issue. The case must be closed if we have any hope of truly helping young people. They must accept the Bible as their inerrant source of information. They may not understand it all. No adult does either. But they must trust its origin and potential for their lives. However, it is healthy to further examine the idea that humans are created (born) with divine purpose. In 2 Chronicles chapter 2, Solomon commences carrying out the construction of the temple as he was instructed by his father, David. Observation of the building process reveals the use of various specific materials and the use of people with various specific skills.

Solomon gave orders to build a temple for the name of the Lord. He conscripted 70,000 men as carriers, 80,000 as stone cutters in the hills, 3,600 as foreman over them. Solomon sent this message to the King of Hiran of Tyre,

> *"Send me a man skilled to work in gold and silver, bronze and iron, purple crimson and blue yarn, ...and experienced*

in the art of engraving to work with my skilled workers whom my father provided".

"I know your servants are skilled in cutting timber". King Hirem replies, "Praise be to the Lord. the God of Israel who made heaven and earth. He has given a wise son endowed with intelligence and discernment. I am sending you Huram Abi, a man of great skill. He is trained to work in gold and silver, bronze and iron, stone and wood and with purple and blue crimson yarn and fine linen. He is experienced in all kinds of engraving and can execute any design given to him."

Several instances listed here indicate training or experience some individuals could have acquired. It has been understood that regardless of one's innate talents, it is possible to acquire a variety of additional skills with training and practice. The theme of this narrative has been to emphasize that each individual created in the image of God has also been gifted with the ability to participate in work designed for him or her. Work refers to activity in which one exerts strength or faculties to perform. Those activities may not be ministerial, yet be divinely purposed. The work can be secular, yet eternal in value if the individual is progressing toward or within a divine call. Case in point, there is nothing ungodly about a young person investing time with the potential to excel in sports or another form of entertainment. God's creation in the physical world clearly indicates that all of His children are not going to be ordained preachers or foreign missionaries, nor might they possess the aptitude to make them fit for some other tasks. Perhaps it would be helpful for mature adults and young people to accept the fact that no one has to possess identical gifts or abilities. We should not evaluate each other's worth or strive for popularity based upon the talents displayed by someone else. We should persuade all young people to value themselves similar to the importance God places on them. With that realization, they should strive to find out what their Creator says about them and discover the gifts He has given them to accomplish His will. We can help them realize that some talents or work may generate wealth or popularity more than other kinds of work. However, if our youth reach spiritual maturity when they understand seeking God's will can produce everything they need to achieve joy and fulfillment, regardless of the popularity, or even the amount of wealth. They should be reminded that many unhappy circumstances exist in the center of millionaire mansions and expensive lifestyles. Of course, poverty and lack are not the goal. Some of God's chosen representatives were very wealthy and some of His most powerful disciples had nowhere to lay their heads.

We talked much about the responsibility that young people have to God who created them. Do young people have a responsibility to themselves, a responsibility that only their Creator can help fulfill?

YOUTH HAVE A RESPONSIBILITY
TO THEMSELVES

Equal is not equity.
Fair may not be equal.
Same is not necessarily fair.

Daniel 1:17 says, *"To these four young men, God gave knowledge and understanding of all kinds of literature and learning and Daniel could understand visions and dreams of all kinds"*. Young people involved in traditional churches have heard the stories of the heroic teenagers, Shadrack, Meshack and Abednego, who were miraculously preserved in the fire furnace because they refused to follow some rules that violated their religious principles. The full story is outlined in chapter 3:19 of Daniel. Even though the rules were established by Nebuchadnezzar, King of Babylon, these young men refused to be intimidated even with the threat of death. There are a couple considerations in the story which call for open debate:

1) If the teenagers were ordered to participate in a legally required activity, are they being disobedient not to follow orders?
2) If they disobeyed a legal mandate from the king, don't they deserve punishment?
3) Is their rebellious act obedience to God and honoring themselves?

These inquiries were not considered in the original framework of the responsibility young people possess toward their divine gifts and ordained purpose. However, it seems appropriate to indicate biblical incidents which may be construed as contradictory. Attempting to delve too deeply into this idea would be an injustice to the objective of this chapter. Hopefully, at a future time, under the guide of spiritual maturity, individuals will be able to reconcile perceived discrepancies within The Bible. The Bible has stood the test of time proving itself to be accurate, holy and inerrant. The inadequate explanation to which this writer can suggest as an experiment debate is the circumstance of the three Hebrew boys. These young men, in their adversity, demonstrate a reality found in a sinful world. The men refuse to follow the king's command. Their decision brings them to a crossroad of obeying God or obeying man. It is at this intersection of conflict that a person must determine his authentic motives. The question is, will one's decision regarding obedience be based upon unadulterated principles? The resolution of psychological conflict will help clarify one's motives. Compliance will rule or dissonance will persist.

In 1 Samuel 10:6, the prophet admonishes Saul, the future king of Israel, *"The spirit of the Lord will come powerfully upon you and will prophesy with them; and you will be changed into a different person"*. Then in 1Samuel 10:7, Samuel continues once these signs are fulfilled, *"Do whatever your hand finds to do, for God is with you (Principles Version)"*.

Dr. Charles Stanley's Life Principles Bible interprets those scriptures in the following manner:

> *It takes the spirit of the living God to turn us into new people, to transform any of us into all He created us to be. This is a transformation the Lord wants for every one of us: Romans 8:28-29, 12:2, 2 Cor. 5:14-21.*

Young people are burdened with tremendous responsibility. The weight of that responsibility varies, depending on the country, culture or family they find themselves in. Some individuals are born into familial circumstances where material advantage is minimal or non-existent. A child born into those circumstances may aspire to do better than what their parents have been able to provide for the family. Depending on the environment, better may be relative. In a country surrounded by object poverty, expectation for what is better, materially, may equate to being able to provide three consistent meals a day, shelter from the elements or safety from life threatening conditions.

In another environment, the expectation for better might be reflected in the ownership of a six figure home rather than a minimum wage in a service job. In some countries, economic strata exist. Economic differences are not the only distinctions among families, which can put pressure on young people. The varying cultural or religious expectations can be just as strenuous. Questions about social life and career can dominate minds and emotions among young people seeking to determine why they exist at this place and time on the planet earth.

Frequently, many written and oral discussions about the purpose of life and the use of or discovery of one's talent are viewed from an American version of success. That success usually has a price tag associated with it. Entertainers, athletes, or even poets are only considered successful after they have achieved status equated to monetary value. Subsequently, few individuals who dedicate their lives to helping others less fortunate than themselves become famous. They certainly fail to acquire the mansion with servants. Even physicians, virtuosos or painters of brilliant art are ignored if their passion is for art's sake, not for financial award. However, it is important to reiterate, especially to young people, that being financially rewarded for using your God given gifts is not wrong at all. Yet, the question posed in this part of the book is what responsibility do young people have to themselves in becoming all that God has created them to be?

I believe what is essential in this discussion of meaning and purpose is to avoid equating life to a dollar bill. There is nothing insignificant about wealth; but is there more? There is nothing necessarily contemptible about being popular, but is there more? There is nothing distasteful about possessing power or position, but is there more? Is there something of equal, maybe greater value? One strategy to reach an answer to these questions is to first determine one's origin. What should one's focus be? What do I owe myself when no one else is around? When neither money, popularity, possession, power or appearance fail to satisfy the longing in my spirit, what is my own responsibility to myself? After all, when no one else is in the room, self will always be present.

Young people should be encouraged to seek wisdom and follow it (Ravi Zacharias). They must learn how to perform. They must learn what to say and what to do. Daniel, chapter 1, comes to mind again in the account of the three Hebrew young men. These young men offered a compromise to their overseer; a compromise they expected to be victorious. However, the compromise eliminated the appearance that they were simply disobeying legitimate authority. They never verbalized total disobedience. Rather, wisdom provided them with what turned out to be a viable alternative. This is what young people owe themselves in light of their lives, their existence, their future, their purpose or eternity. It isn't surprising that a significant number of unchurched young people are skeptical about the truth and accuracy of the Bible. Unfortunately, there are even churched and unchurched individuals of the same mind. This is critically important. Young people who lack respect for the clear teachings of the Bible may be denying themselves the opportunity to know truth and gain wisdom. This is even a challenge to professing believers; what they believe about God, His power, His power, His sovereignty and purpose for the human race.

Young people owe it to themselves to establish the truth. They have to perform a kind of "reality test", sort of like the Gideon fleece experiment. Many individuals may have trouble accepting that incident as believable. In Judges 36-40, God sent an angel to tell Gideon that since he was strong and courageous, he had been called by God to lead His people into battle and conquer the Mennonites. Keeping Gideon, was at that time already in hiding from those many enemy bullies. So, Gideon's response to the angel was, "Oh boy, do you have the wrong guy? You must have gotten my address confused with someone else". The angel had insisted that there had been no mistake, Gideon was indeed the mighty man of God that the message described.

Not wanting to appear disrespectful, the angelic being Gideon said, *"I need to be sure that you are talking about the right person. If you are really from God and if my God really, really wants me to take this job, here is a proposition. I am going to place this piece of fleece from a sheep on the ground. If God wants me to do this, ask God if I leave this fleece on the ground all night, by morning I want the fleece to be dry and the ground around it to be soaked and wet"*. The angel accepted Gideon's condition on behalf of God. So, the fleece lay on the ground all night. By morning, the fleece was bone dry; not even a drop of dew touched it.

Not to be outdone, Gideon still had reservations and doubts. He asked the angel, *"Let's try one more thing. Just to be sure you're still not making a mistake, let's leave the fleece on the ground one more night. This time in the morning, let the fleece be soaked and wet, but let the ground around it be bone dry"*. The angel, speaking on God's behalf replied, "Okay". The next morning, Gideon anxiously ran to check the fleece. It was completely water logged as if it had been soaked in a tub of water, but when Gideon examined the ground around the fleece, there was not even a dew drop. Consequently, Gideon stepped out on faith and demonstrated to be one of the greatest military leaders that the nation of Israel ever had. God gave him time to work out his fears and doubts, nevertheless, God created him for a specific task. Had he continued to refuse, who knows what the outcome would have been for him or the nation of Israel.

This is a suitable object lesson. The God who created you not only minds you checking out His credentials and using a fleecing technique. He will help you deal with your anxieties about what He has called you to do. However, as a young person, you owe it to yourself to find out if He is legit. Merely having an opinion about Him is insufficient. It is important that you read what He says about Himself. Listen to what others who are familiar with Him say about Him. Then, run your own fleece experiment but maybe not with a real piece of lamb's wool. Don't insult God, but talk to Him. Ask Him questions and He will respond. He is not intimidated by your questions. The Bible does say, *"...and you shall know the truth ...and the truth shall set you free"*. You may be saying, "I don't know what to do with my life". God's word says, *".. and I can do all things through Christ who gives me strength (Phil. 4:13)"*. God's word abides forever, you only have a lifetime on this earth to accomplish what you have been created to do. Psalms 90:12 reminds you, *"Teach us to number our days that we may gain a heart of wisdom"*. To demonstrate wisdom and use time wisely, young people have to seek the mind of God. You need knowledge and wisdom. Only God can answer what He has for you to do in life. You owe that to yourself. Undoubtedly, young people have a responsibility to themselves to investigate the possible impact that God and His plans have on their lives. Especially, since influence could be manifested in critical ways.

First, let's consider the impact of God's direction on a young person's moral life. We have considered ideas thus far through a somewhat spiritual lens. Even though the spiritual viewpoint permeates all of one's life or behavior. Let's look more specifically at right and wrong behavior; perhaps even healthy versus unhealthy consequences. We are aware of the current debate in our society between appropriate actions compared to inappropriate actions. Even though the Bible is not so complimentary, it does express concern about behaviors which can contribute to self-harm or even self-destruction.

I propose that young people have a responsibility to themselves to review God's concerns for moral behavior and consequences for immoral behavior. With the goal of limiting what sounds like personal attacks, let's limit the definition of morality to the mental and emotional attitudes of an individual toward a task. This is an objective examination that hopefully will not distract from the main idea of this deliberation.

There are some lifestyles quite prevalent among individuals and groups that might be considered immoral. For example, without highlighting complete ideas, consider stealing from others, lying about someone in an attempt to damage their reputation or just to gain an undeserved advantage. Without hesitation, I confess that reference to immoral behavior of young people does not imply that older people are less guilty. Unfortunately, much of the immoral behavior has been inherited from the older individuals. Other behaviors of questionable value include consuming or selling illegal substances to be used for recreation or psychological escape. Some of these behaviors lead to violence, sexual promiscuity and revenge (settling the score). All of these behaviors demonstrate interest and exaltation of self. The problem is that their ultimate resolution is physical destruction, conflict with legal authority, sickness, ruination of one's name or reputation. Rarely do these behaviors leave their participants in better condition. The results are more often destitution, regret or sorrow.

I cannot suggest that the Bible or any other resource will prevent young people from making mistakes or getting caught up in devastation beyond their control. The evidence of lives lived by many offers a picture that adds favor to those who listen to or follow the lessons outlined in a book, supposedly designed by a Creator, for those He created. Young people owe themselves an opportunity to examine the veracity of a record that took hundreds of years to write with contributions from over 40 writers. Each writer's perspective is consistent with the writer before him!

It has been articulated by various individuals that had every physical problem, i.e. physical in terms of its existence in the concrete world of seeing, hearing and touching had a spiritual basis. This suggests that the root of some problems human beings deal with in the physical world originate in the sphere of spiritual relationships. For example, a young person who disobeys his or her parents and engages in various immoral behavior has a serious problem in his relationship with God and with spiritual responsibility or understanding. Ephesians specifically reminds young people to obey (respect) their parents because it is right. In chapter 4, it also teaches people to live in the futility of their thinking, *"... that they are darkened in the understanding and separated from the life of God because of the ignorance that is in them due to the hardening of their hearts,....Having lost all their sensitivity, they have given themselves over to sensuality so as to indulge in every kind of impurity and they are full of greed"*. These words are warnings and admonishments that our young people owe themselves to see if they can gain wisdom about how to care for their lives physically, morally, mentally and emotionally.

Trying to be the best person one can be is not only a responsibility to one's Creator, that responsibility extends to our ancestors and posterity. What do we owe to our ancestors? In many cultures around the world, children are reared in an atmosphere of ancestor worship. They perform religious ceremonies to seek wisdom for decisions and guidance. In many of these cultures, serious repercussions can derive from disrespecting elders or symbols which represent ancestors. These societies spend much time teaching the young about the heroic or incredible sustainability of the ancestors, events which contributed to the survival of the tribe or race.

The Bible does not teach the kind of worship of patriarchs or matriarchs. The Bible does throughout demonstrate the importance of honoring mothers and fathers as well as the names of those God first used to establish the nation of Israel. It also describes the honor and respect He demands from those whom He has created and continues to provide for.

What is perhaps more important for modern youth to consider apart from paying due homage to our Creator is illustrating appreciation for the people God used over the years to bring us to our current existence. Some ancestors made tremendous sacrifices to hold on to what they felt was valuable to the future race. Many of them worked extremely hard and even offered their health or lives. Young people should recognize, as their origin, their true source of help in any situation. They should also honor and respect their parents or those who serve in that role to provide necessary substance for their survival; even if the substance is less than elaborate. The implication is that everyone has derived from someone else and somewhere. Therefore, it seems reasonable that one contribution to those who have contended before us should be appreciated by doing the very best with what we have presently. Whether we consider talents, gifts or material resources, a foundation somewhere in the past provided something for us to stand on. We are obligated to exert our best effort in appreciation to those from whom we have descended. One pulling himself up by his own bootstraps is such a ruse and unlikely probability. That kind of arrogance is unhealthy to the general society and contributes to undeserved notions of superiority.

As young people are advised to live their best in honor of themselves and ancestors, there is perhaps a responsibility to those who follow them. Why should young people give consideration to posterity? As outdated as the concept sounds, those who exist now are the progeny of ancestors, recent or long gone. Essentially, the advantages or disadvantages we currently experience in some way are associated with our forebears. Unless the current youth expect Armageddon to transpire during their lifetime, there should be an awareness or at least an expectation that the world, our communities and environment should be better than when we found it.

One way to invest in the future is to make sure you are living up to your own potential and purpose. As we benefit from inventions and ideas generated by our ancestors, we can be glad that they did not squander their talents. In the current superhighways and fast paced city traffic, the traffic light is a precious commonplace lifesaver. The discovery of Penicillin is especially popular during a period of epidemics and pandemics. Other medical marvels and ingenious modes of travel, communication and exploration demonstrates the self discipline and persistence required of individuals who labored to materialize ideas that emanated from their minds. Should not each person strive for the same? To search out the singular purpose or purposes for which one is born into a certain historical period possessing certain talents for that time. A question raised by Ester's uncle, Mordecai, in Ester 4:14, *"And who knows whether thou art not come to the kingdom for such a time as this? For if thou holdest thy peace at this time, then shall relief and deliverance arise from another place"*. Ester was in a unique position as queen to save her people from destruction, however, to approach the king without his permission or request could mean death. Her uncle reminded her that if she kept quiet, she might save herself, but God would use someone else to carry out His plan to save the Jewish nation. She would miss her opportunity of carrying out the purpose for which had been born. Instead of her being remembered as a Judge of Israel, she perhaps would be remembered in an infamous way. This is a decision young people are frequently faced with. What should I do with my abilities or my opportunities? The answer lies in God's word and within the counsel of godly people. I repeat, the fact that each individual created is much too valuable to appear on earth for no purpose. The complexity of the mind and body, the spirit and creativity suggest purpose and capacity to achieve something special. Should young people hunger to see, apart from the physical body, what a supernatural Creator has placed within you. What has He created you to do? They should also have the confidence that once He has shown you your purpose, He will provide everything you need to accomplish it.

Consequences for what we do can reach beyond us. Wrong behavior always hurts others. Our behavior can mean hardship and desolation for generations to come. Similarly, disobedience and positive steps can mean blessings and benefits for our descendants (Genesis 17:5-8, 1 Kings 15:11; 2 Kings 18: 1,3; 2 Chronicles 17:3, 34:1-3, <u>Charles Stanley Life Principles Bible</u>, 2017).

Youth Must Realize
There is No Whining,
No Qutting, No
Dropping out of
the Game!

The goal of young people must be to do everything they can with the gifts or talents they have been given. I understand the debate generated by the conflict among individuals who expose evolution of men and those who believe in creation. Obviously, the content of this book reflects my confidence in creation and a sovereign, all powerful Creator. Let's allow for unbiased exchange for a short period of time. There are a couple of undisputed facts worthy of unbiased consideration. The first fact for young people to observe is that they are alive in a human body which possesses intellect and various physical potential. These attributes can be utilized for meaningful purposes or be ignored and unused. Another irrefutable fact is that you're going to die. Young people who are physically healthy often have difficulty imagining the termination of their physical existence. Unfortunately, for many of us who are no longer "young" realize too late how much of that youth is being wasted and cannot be restored. Those who are still young have an opportunity to spare themselves untold remorse by obtaining an early understanding of the value and ephemeral quality of youth. Except for those who, through no fault of their own, come into this worldly existence with similar potential and capacity. However, we must admit that in many parts of the world, including the United States, many individuals born with tremendous potential are unable to maximize their ability because of inequities, biases and limitations imposed upon them by other individuals or institutions. Nevertheless, even with various unwanted limitations, many individuals overcome restrictions and excel to the limits of their potential. Young people who are free to strive to reach their potential without undue hindrances must understand why they have nothing to whine about. Whine is a rather archaic term for many of today's youth. It is freely used by people of certain generations to describe infantile complaining by persons who have no apparent rationale to do so.

Young people must be honest with themselves and examine "Do I really have anything to complain about"? Experiencing difficulty is no reason to whine. Resistance from unexpected forces is no rationale to complain, especially if there is a possibility that each person has a special talent that can be used to improve the world one lives in. After all, the shadow of mortality will eventually remind you how fleeting life is. Whether creationism or evolution is the position one accepts, it will not add time to one's existence on this earth. Sooner or later death appears. So, the reality is, no one benefits from whining. The prevailing question may be, "Did I utilize the potential that I had? Did I serve a meaningful purpose?". However, Creationism will ask, "Did you achieve and were you obedient to the purpose for which you were created?".

In various cultures of the world, young people are under exceptional pressure to achieve academically and financially for the benefit of the family. Failure to achieve at this superior level often pressures youngsters to take their lives. They are accused of bringing shame on the families. Then, there are other cultures where it is understood that one's talent or potential is irrelevant. One's economic or social status is predetermined by law and history. They are recorded experiences where individuals who are born into a "substandard" status fail to progress above the historical status mentally, even though they have moved to a different country where the previous social strata is not practiced or enforced. It might be unbalanced to refer to the social strata practice in certain countries without acknowledging the impact of the religious belief embedded in the culture of those societies. It is a caste system which reinforces the inferiority of some people and the superiority of others based upon their heritage.

If a behavior is practiced long enough, it becomes normal and expected. The possibility that thousands, perhaps millions of talented individuals show limited to inferior performance in their lives merely because others deemed them inferior is troubling. One might question what inventions, medical advances or priceless works of art and beauty wasted away, buried under fear and subservience spirits.

Fortunately, no such laws are officially practiced in most Western or European countries. As indicated earlier, we are aware of historical practices and attitudes which can or do interfere with certain young people reaching their greatest potential. At this writing, hopefully, there are few of those practices currently supported by legal mandates.

Throughout the years, there seems to be ideas and preferences which generate conflict between the younger generations and the older generations. Frequently, the more mature individuals, including parents, fear for the survival of the young. Those perceptions are often based upon unorthodox behaviors and decision making methods applied by the young. However, no matter how foreign the strategies utilized, the members of the younger generation manage to survive or even thrive. This inevitably may be ascribed to providence, luck or nature. Many may note that the world has been in existence a long time. Life seems to merely go on. That Cavalier view supports the question of, "the world is still here, why should I worry about trying to accomplish anything significant while I am in this world?". The response to that idea might be, one never knows when things might change. Let us conjecture that there is a final day, even if it is your final day, but you never applied yourself to do your best at anything in particular. Even more broadly, what if you failed to identify your purpose in this world? That could leave a gaping hole in one's legacy or provide you with an earth shaking shock if you are mistaken about the afterlife.

Similar to older people of the past, I am concerned for youth trying to survive in antagonistic environments. Spiritual forces, emotional and psychological forces, even financial pressures encourage some young people to voice their discontent and doubt about the possible existence of a compassionate Creator. They also lack confidence in the possibility that they can have a life of fulfillment, purpose or joy. Many resign to merely survive the storms of life until their final days on earth.

This author lived in an urban, single parent home for a while. Another time, sharecropping with relatives on a tenant farm was our life. I concluded that young people must not complain nor quit. Neither should they get out of the game of life.

Colossians 3:23-24 advises, *"and whatever you do, do it heartily as to the Lord, and not unto men. Knowing that of the Lord you shall receive the reward of the inheritance for you serve the Lord Christ"*. Verse 25 continues, *"But he that doeth wrong shall receive for the wrong which he hath done and there is no respect of persons"*. The preceding directives address the expectation to demonstrate moral and social character towards others. This attitude should exemplify toward superiors (employers, parents, etc.) or a counterpart (co-worker, classmate, etc.). It is evident that certain individuals who adhere to spiritual principles are expected to demonstrate justice or experience repercussions from God who we represent.

Another idea which should be harnessed by young people is that the best effort should always be displayed when performing any task, regardless of how anyone else is behaving.

Youth Must Realize There is No Dropping Out of The Game!

Someone who feels confident about his purpose requires little supervision simply because his goal is to always perform well in the eyes of his Creator. This perspective also compels an individual to persist in the face of difficulty. The only responsibility you have is to be obedient by doing your best, beyond that, the consequences are out of your hands. Perhaps, some young people put too much on their shoulders. In this high pressure environment, in some countries, to succeed professionally or materially at all cost, the weight can be unbearable. Sustained emotional and even physical pressure may eventually deplete our human capacity to sustain that negativity. This is why it seems that young people, for their own survival, should investigate quite seriously, if there is a Creator who has literally designed them for a specific purpose on this place called Earth. If that conclusion is affirmative, will it not release hundreds or thousands of young people from the frustration of failing to rise to the expectations of so many people? Peer pressure would lose its meaning. Success would be relegated to its proper place of relativity and even failure would lose its power as a concept. Each person would notice only what must be accomplished according to their talents, interests and longevity. All of these factors dictated and provided by someone who will lead with all knowledge and concern for his creation's well being. This would be little explanation to whine. There is no purpose to quit or drop out of life, figuratively or literally.

I detect a contradiction in my mind and spirit. I believe the Bible is the truthful, inerrant Word of God. This source of my contradiction is, God does all things well. I am also compelled to defend that God is no respecter of persons. These truths communicate the equality, though not sameness which He distributes to human creation. This distribution may be manifested in innate mental, physical, emotional or even spiritual capacity. This understanding of God's justice feeds my inability to accept the ongoing discrepancy between the implied superiority of one group of children over another when performing mental tasks. Apart from cultural, environmental, or educational experiences which can be reflected in these differences, I find no other alternative but to question either the verity of the Bible or the integrity of my God. Neither option is viable for my sanity or spiritual stability.

GOD APPROVED;
WHY LABEL ME?

The notion of this book pivots around several key truths, which can help youth people live fulfilling lives. One of those truths is "God is sovereign". As such His sovereignty emanates from His position as Creator. He has the right of creatorship. Genesis chapter 1 indicates He is the Creator of heaven and earth. Colossians chapter 1 reiterates His authority delegated to the son, *"For by Him were all things created, that are in heaven and that are in the earth, visible and invisible, whether they be thrones or dominions, or principalities or powers: all things were created by Him and for Him"*. The precursor to that declaration in Genesis 1:31 affirms, *"And God saw everything that He had made, and behold, it was very good"*.

We are reminded of another truth: everything God creates is "good". Everything and "everyone" falls into that category. The question rises, "If everyone God creates is good, why is so much bad carried out in the world?". The answer may sound antithetical. Some may purport that the Bible is contradictory. However, the Bible is truthful and verifiable. God creates life. Life occurs prior to a human being experiencing birth. Life generated by God existed prior to the now sinful nature inherited from the man, Adam. As God told Jeremiah, "Before I formed you in your mother's womb, I knew you". God's creation of Jeremiah existed before the DNA of his parents contributed to the color of his eyes, his bone structure or his height. God knew him, created him before the potential for misbehavior invaded his physical body or mind. Subsequently, Moses can still verify that, "And God saw everything that He had made, and behold, it was very good". Clearly the curse of sin contributing to evil behavior is inherited before birth but after pure creation. There are Bible scholars more noted and surely more theologically qualified to debate this question. My only contention is that God does not create anything which is not good. Every individual is good for what they were created to be or do. They are perhaps even parents whose confusion is encased in the sadness of their child, who from childhood to presently twenty-one years old, are unable to manage their basic human needs. The final words of The Bible change not, "Behold it was very good; good for the purpose for which he or she was created". To understand purpose may require spending much time communing with and listening to God. Nevertheless, each created is for a purpose to be fulfilled during their time on this earth. He also provides each person with the gifts or talents necessary to accomplish their God given purposes. This explains why true fulfillment derives from individuals aligning their lives with the purpose for which they were created. Once an individual has taken that vital step, the consequences become all of God's responsibility. If young people can capture that truth, they will realize that no matter what anyone says about them, they are "God approved". If God has approved them upon their creation, why should anyone else be permitted to label me? They were created by the same God who created everyone else. Young people can recognize that some others are born with different abilities, different gifts or circumstances. Many times those various circumstances help to create advantages for one person over another. Yet, the truth maintains that God is the Creator of all. Subsequently, no individual is created with greater value than another. All emanate from the same dust, however, molded from God's hands and in His image. Psalms 103 says, *"He remembers that we are dust"*. This knowledge on God's part stimulates compassion on our behalf and patience. Perhaps young people might apply similar sentiment toward each other rather than condemning oneself or bullying each other. They are all God approved.

So, why label me unattractive? Why label me unintelligent? Why label me useless? There may be some behaviors I have emulated from my home environment or my own simple nature. The same One who created me knows how to correct the problems. It may take some time but parents, educators and Christians, I am God approved. You should stop labeling me, I will.

Among the pages of this book, several spiritual principles have been recorded. Two are worth repeating. The first is young people should seriously consider that they have been created for a purpose. Secondly, their creation and purpose were derived prior to their birth. Thirdly, every individual has equal value in the eyes of a sovereign God. Finally, and of tremendous importance, God does all things well. He is no respecter of persons. The concepts of equality, equity and purpose necessitate broader review.

Unbiblical Inundation of Special Education Programs in Public Schools

I deliberated a long time trying to determine how or if the sensitive topic of special education should be addressed in this record. I also concerned myself about the possible misconceptions various individuals or groups might extrapolate.

Special education in public schools has been a sensitive topic for years in the education of students in America. Indeed, it observes all of the attention it has obtained. The lives of many precious youngsters can be impacted by decisions, programs and philosophies from numerous people .

Generally, special education is a term which acquired official usage in the education lexicon around 1971 in the United States. The passage of the All American Disabilities Act opened the door to obtain a free and public education equal to every other student.

Many people might agree that special education generally describes unique programs specifically developed for individual students (IEP's) who have been identified. The needs may be psychological in nature, physical or mental if it hinders the child's normal learning opportunities.

Strict federal and state laws impose detailed enforcement under the penalty of law for violations for the protection of the special needs students. The process utilized to determine a child's qualification is extensive and particular. The creation of various laws supporting the special education programs and process allegedly protect the rights of all students. This is a theory which is lofty and appropriate when we observe the number of lives which can be impacted over a normal 12 year public school experience. Support for these programs are vitally important and needed for some students. However, there are educational researchers who challenge the negative connotation of special education as generally applied. These researchers opine that technically gifted and talented programs are also "special education" programs. They extend the view that special education primarily refers to students either falling on the below average on a normal curve of intelligence. The gifted and talented students translate without any negative connotation. This distinction exists even though special education within the legal area fails to restrain special needs to limit mental capacity. Mental capacity can certainly be allowed as a criteria. There is also evidence which demonstrates highly intelligent individuals portraying unusual levels of distractibility, impatience and temperamental extremes who may qualify for special education services to help them achieve success among the normal educational curricular.

By now, one might wonder why special education is a topic of discussion. This is a book about young people's view of their creation and purpose and the fact that God does all things well. In Genesis 1 and 2, numerous explanations refer to how God felt about His earthly creatures and it was good. Then in Psalm 139:13-16:

> *13 For you created my innermost being, You knit me together in my mother's womb.*

> *14 I praise You because I am fearfully and wonderfully made. Your works are wonderful. I know that full well.*

> *15 My frame was not hidden from You when I was made in a secret place, when I was woven together in the depths of the earth.*

> *16 Your eyes saw my unformed body; all the days ordained for me were written in Your book before they came to be.*

Clearly, the preceding scripture reasserts God's foreknowledge, creation and pre-ordained purpose for each of His creations. In Christian circles, young people are encouraged to seek God's wisdom and direction for their lives. The question is, is this advice reserved only for certain young people? As Christians, are some of us still debating the idea of monogenesis (one source of human creation) and polygenesis (one creation for the white race and a different creation gave rise to a darker race)? Instead, some of us settle on the curse of Ham as an explanation of the social economic distinctions observed between students of color and white students. Oppressive movements and policies hinging on different versions of eugenics have for centuries served as the foundation for ignoring these disadvantages experienced by certain children who spend their existence coping with the shortcomings of perceived inferiority. As Dr. W.E. Dubois related, *"This American world yields no true self-consciousness, but only lets him see himself through the revelation of the other world. This sense of always looking at one's self through the eyes of others, of measuring one's soul by the tape of a world that looks on in amused contempt and pity. One ever feels his two-ness"*.

Even as many people survived and overcame this cognitive dissonance, there have been courageous spokespersons who presented logic ahead of convenience or bias against people of color. In May 1906, Jewish professor Franz Boas spoke at the Atlantic University conference on The Health and Physique of the Negro-American. During that time, scholars questioned or rejected the widely held impression that the races were biologically distinct. Dr. Boas was an eminent anthropologist from Columbia University. To those who maintained the theory of inferiority of the "Negro race", Dr. Boas explained the past history of black race does not support that statement. Boas shocked many attendees at the conference by recounting the stories of precolonial West African kingdoms like Chana, Mali, and Songhai. Dr. Boas awakened many on that day to the historical evidence that Africans possessed superb history in the sciences, mathematics, economics and scholarship long before the Americas existed. Dr. Boas's presentation debunked the political position that it was the "white man's burden" to resolve the darker race from ignorance, heathenism and poverty.

Dr. Boas' viewpoint years ago is more consistent with the view espoused and substantiated in the Bible. Even if there were some accuracy to the theories like the curse of Ham in Genesis 5:32, the fact that the success of African civilizations were subsequent to the proposed curse seemingly would be sufficient evidence to denounce such a biased interpretation. However, if this was not sufficient to divorce oneself from a frivolous viewpoint. Christian believers might accept the commitment from God in Deuteronomy 24:16 that the sins of the father would no longer be passed on to the children. Again, this conclusion is much more consistent with the God of the Bible who is just and compassionate.

Yours truly is a veteran educator who lacks medical training, particularly in brain research. Yet, important questions persist in this writer's mind. Question #1, Of the children diagnosed with a learning deficit in need of immediate structured improvement, would the conclusion be less frequent if clinicians and teachers imagined their own children at the end of the process? The second question - are the critical decisions too subjective; rarely consulting with a higher power who is the original designer? If so, it would be logical for spirituality to assume influence, if not control, of the conversation. I do not desire to confuse spirituality with religiosity. However, I suggest that the crux of the decision should be Bible based. For example, Genesis 1:1 states, *"In the beginning God created the heavens and the earth,"*. The remainder of that chapter highlights how God created other entities and declared them good (complete, fully able to their purpose) such as the stars, moon, day, night and firmament. These are enduring creations. God labels even the inanimate creations, "very good". This reference is subjective, however, in the beginning, no other opinion mattered. By the end of the chapter, one God has completed His work and certified all as complete and approved.

We reach Genesis 3:7. It announces that God, the only one with perfect knowledge, *"formed man of the dust of the ground and breathed into his nostrils the breath of life; and man became a living being"*. God declared all of His creation prior to man "good". It appears reasonable that the creation formed in His own image would also enter into existence "good". If that is accurate, the next creation in Genesis 2:22 might deserve to be called "very, very good". This is the scenario where the copy might be better than the original, at least in appearance. In verse 22 of Genesis, from the rib which the Lord God had taken from man, He made into a woman and brought her to the man. She too was complete, perfect for her position and function in the fully furnished Garden of Eden.

At this juncture, many people are familiar with the description of Satan's destructive effect on God's perfect world and innocent human couple. Consequently, it led to the disruption and cursed existence of all future humans descending from Adam and Eve. These descendants would be born with a proclivity toward wrong thinking, destructive behavior and even imperfect mental capacity. Some of this curse may also be reflected in some physical attributes. This confession is most assuredly reflected among children born with inabilities in some or all learning domains. What defies biblical explanation is the disproportionate number of children in public schools who are "classified" lacking mental capacity to learn or perform at sufficient academic levels. Another disconcerting observation is that the disproportional percentage of those students are children of color, students of similar races and backgrounds. To express the theme clearly, "Too frequently the majority of students placed into public school education programs are either African American, Hispanic or economically poor".

However, it is possible that many of those students come from urban or poor rural communities. Many of these environments lack exposure to formal educated foundations including language skills or mathematical/problem solving principles. This lack of exposure promotes a deficit on experimental experience. The environment does not decrease mental capacity.

Another conundrum provokes greater contradictions. According to a study reported by John Hopkins University in Maryland, only 4 % of students who enter special education programs by 4th grade even test out by the end of their 12th grade year. Following such results, it is evident that progress has not achieved much on the investment. Over 40 years since The American with Disabilities Act, the results have not been impressive for most children. A 4% success rate is sub performance on almost any rate of assessment. With such a dismal rate of success, it begs to question why most of these special education programs remain without being pressured to demonstrate greater success.

There is another statistic which is relevant to the question rate of success among our students in special education. Unless there is a skewed sample of population, it does not add up that from God's original creation of man and woman, there is a disruption or deduction of God's sustaining spirit today.

I am aware that there are sincere believers who would offer that, just because God is no respecter of persons does not defend that God created every person with equal ability in everything. I concede the apparent logic and proof of this position. There is even a broad promise which God makes to David that can be applied universally. In 1 Kings 2, David consoles his son Solomon, *"..so be strong, act like a man and observe what the Lord requires: Walk in obedience to Him and keep His decrees and commands, his laws and regulations. Do this so that you may prosper in all you do and wherever you go..."*. Clearly, this is a conditional promise with unlimited possibility. If we teach our youth of their creative value, their boundless potential and preordained purpose, we provide an opportunity for them to know their power, including He who has all power. Jeremiah 1:5 says, *"Before I formed you in the womb, I knew you. Before you were born, I set you apart. I appointed you"*.

Many young people live in frustration, fear or doubt. The word of God specifically expresses that exercise is superfluous. He determined your purpose prior to your birth or beginning. The challenge is the necessity of nurturing a relationship with one's creator that permits those purposes to be revealed. If so much care and specificity has been enacted to create a being of purpose in the image of the creator, would the creator not also anticipate the abilities and talents required to carry out the tasks in this world?

In this scripture, God is talking to Jeremiah. Would it not be reasonable to conclude that the message is universal to all men and women. If this is a priori assumption, it is reasonable for one to conclude that all of us originate with purpose and mission. This suggestion points to created potential, created purpose and Divine Connection.

For battle, David had 37 mighty men of war. Joseb-Basshebeth raised his spear against 800 men whom he killed in one encounter. Eleazer struck down so many Philistines alone until his hand grew tired and froze to the sword. Shammah stood in the middle of a field of lentils and defended the land alone. Kabzeel went down into a pit on a snowy day and killed a lion. Also, he struck down an Egyptian giant with the giant's own spear. In the tribe of Benjamin there were 700 warriors expert with the sling in either right or left hand.

When Solomon was preparing to build and furnish the Temple at Jerusalem, he brought Huram from Tyre. Huram, like his father, was a skilled craftsman in bronze. He was filled with wisdom by God with understanding and knowledge to do all kinds of bronze work (1 Kings 7:13-14). Workers at the quarry prepared the blocks for the temple so that no hammer, chisel or other tool could be heard being used at the site of the temple. King Hiram of Tyre had men cut cedar and Juniper logs from Lebanon to build the temple. The logs had to be shipped via the Mediterranean Sea. Solomon "conscripted" 30 thousand men from all Israel (over 13 years to complete the building of the temple).

The clan and families were responsible for carrying the frames of the portable tabernacle, its crossbars, posts and bases. They were also to carry the bases of tabernacle, pegs, rope and all the equipment related to the tabernacle. When building the Tabernacle, God instructed those who were skilled to come and make everything the Lord commanded.

"...tent, covering, clasps, frames, crossbars, posts, bases, ark needed poles and _____ cover, curtain and shields, lampstand, lamps and oil for light, the altar of incense with its poles, incense altar, curtain for the doorway, etc. bronze basin, woven garments for ministering in the sanctuary, sacred garments for Aaron the priest, Every skilled woman spun with her hands...blue, purple or scarlet yarn or fine linen. Women who were willing and had the skill spun the goat hair (Exodus 35-4). Exodus 36 records, "So every skilled person to whom the Lord has given skill and ability to know how to carry out all the work of constructing the sanctuary is to do the work as the Lord commanded. Further

in chapter 36:8, Moses records "All those who were skilled among the workers made the tabernacle with curtains and linen by expert hands".

I am aware that the story of Exodus lights the events, relationship and interaction of God and the Israelites. However, it is also clear that those outside of the chosen people (foreigners) participated in the journey and experience of the 40 year excursion. Scripture does not designate any race of people devoid of inherent skill due to their race or ethnicity. The scripture frequently indicates the proclivity of some races toward certain abilities or another. However, these distinctions point to cultural differences and geographical or survival needs, not due to Godly curse. We can also expect that within certain cultures, there are manifestations of superior skills among individuals.

There are Christian advocates who challenge whether the disproportionate representation of one race of children in special education programs is a spiritual matter. Really? Perhaps some from this school of thought succumbed to the theory that dark skinned people sadly are under the curse of Noah's son Ham. Surely such a curse would explain the natural occurrence of slavery in America. It would also explain, or at least justify, why some educators have low expectations for certain children of color. That rationale would further provide credence to why more educators and communities are not outraged that after more than 40 years, special education programs in public schools continue to grow rather than diminish. Twenty percent to sixty percent of the students in these programs are children of color, primarily African-American and Latino. In many urban school districts, that range may be 70% to 80% of the student population, receiving some form of special education services.

In a book focused on God and His capability, why or how does special education align with the narrative? Well, the response is "He (God) does all things well". This title does not make an exception for God's ability or view. Actually, it is more than a title; it is a declaration based on God Himself. All is pretty inclusive, wouldn't you say? If God affirms this testimony about Himself, who are we to declare to certain children "God does all things well but you have some flaw". In which case, God is no longer the "All things well God". Instead, He becomes a "Respecter of Persons". He does all things well for certain people and not for others. Please understand that naivety is not one of my flaws. I have many others but that is not one of them. For clarity, I repeat, there are individuals born with physical or mental characteristics which make learning and achieving under usual circumstances very difficult. We also accept that even with exceptional support systems, some individual's disabilities are too difficult to compensate for. Emphasis is on the word "individuals". My concern is the proportion of children from certain races which are assigned to special education programs. The assignments are human determined as are the criteria. I do not believe God makes any mistakes. I believe that whomever He grants life to is placed on the earth for a purpose.

I am not inclined to determine what that purpose is. However, when God's resume expresses that He does all things well, and as repeated frequently in Genesis, "He......and it was good". He approved of what He made, including me and others. So, when do some creatures acquire the authority to label other creatures "not approved"? Why are we labeling children year after year with no noticeable improvement in their performance? Yet, we keep sending them back to the same teachers doing the same thing for 12 years. For some teachers, the continuation becomes job security. There is nothing distasteful about security. Without exception, it should be rewarded for a job well done. This has become a contrary issue. Too many students are investing hours of their young lives without benefit to their futures.

Since the Bible has served as a base of reference, let's examine additional scripture which seem to reflect God's sovereignty in the lives of humans as well as His predetermined design. "Before I formed you in the womb, I knew you. Before you were born, I set you apart. I appointed you as a profit to the nations (NIV, Jer. 1:6)". It is very easy to conclude that God's designation and purpose was exceptional in this case, structured only for the prophet Jeremiah, for the special work he was called to perform". This interpretation would not be in error. The error I am afraid would exist in limited God's sovereignty and ability to exercise such specificity and preparation for each individual, yours truly included. As highlighted already in Genesis, God commands, *"Let us make mankind in our image, in our likeness so that they may rule over the fish in the sea and the birds in the sky, over livestock and all the wild animals, and over all the creatures that move along the ground (Gen. 1:26, NIV)".* So, God created mankind in His own image, in the image of God He created them, male and female He created them. I am aware that this is the 21st century. A couple of proclamations of that scripture feed controversy. That is not the purpose of this narrative. I do not shy away from controversy. I propose confronting one major bite of this biblical elephant at this time. The presumption that I lift up for consideration is that mankind has been created to rule (manage, control) all animate and inanimate creations that God has placed in this world. It appears to me that, for mankind to successfully carry out his/her responsibility, the Creator had to instill the inherent talents and abilities. Managing the sea requires certain types of skills or proclivities. Managing the creatures that move along the ground requires a different temperament and skill set. Managing the birds in the sky and wild animals call for a different preference. Even managing human beings demand different personality traits, levels of understanding, patience and emotional stability than someone who overseeing birds. According to Jeremiah 1:6, God crafted the personality, human relations components, oratorical skills and spiritual discernment within Jeremiah before he was born. Do normal, everyday Christians assume God does not do the same for us? That is, if the Bible is without error. We can also concede that many individuals are either born with multiple talents and natural inclination while others can acquire various skills via training or observation. That capacity aligns with being made in the image of God. He is intelligent. Intelligence can be applied with effort to master many skills. Even an environmental or cultural environment can introduce and refine certain skills with effort. Nevertheless, it is my belief that every individual is created and carries within his DNA the expressed purpose for which he is brought into this world. One case in point, even though this may not be the most apropos example: the 3 servants in Matthew 25:1-29 were entrusted with various amounts of money while the master went away. One servant had 5 bags of gold, a second had 2 bags of gold and the third servant had 1 bag of gold. Even if the view (is often advocated) that the servants received what the master determined they could handle, no limit was established regarding the maximum that each servant could have accumulated. Greater industriousness from he was given one talent could also have achieved as much as he achieved with 10 talents. It seems that the master's anger with the servant was due to laziness and slothfulness, or even lack of faith. There is no verification that there was a distraction among their innate capability, rather initiative is indicated.

Since Christian believers are encouraged to read this book, it is necessary to confront the misperception Ham, one of Noah's sons, was cursed when he reported to his older brothers about seeing his father's nakedness. Noah, accordingly from waking from his drunken stupor, cursed his youngest son. According to Lange's commentary, "his youngest son" actually had four sons. Canaan was the youngest son. Ham was the third son. The curse was apparently applied to Canaan rather than Ham. The curse did not apply to black people. Note the descendant Noah's four sons:

Cush- *the progenitors of the Ethiopians*
Mizriam-*of the Egyptians*
Phut- *of the Libyans and people of Africa*
Canaan- *of the Canaanites*

Thus the curse was leveled at Canaan and not Phut (who may have founded the African nations). There exist no racial implications whatsoever within the curse. The problem concerning the Canaanites was not in the color of their skin but rather in the condition of their hearts. In fact, the skin texture of the Israelites and Canaanites at the time of Joshua's invasion was probably very similar. Arthur C. Constance, renowned scholar and anthropologist writes:

"In the case of Ham and his descendants, history shows that Ham rendered on extraordinary service to mankind from the point of view of the physical developments of civilization (Willmington's Guide to the Bible, pg.34)"

With the theory of inherent inferiority of black people debunked as a curse from God, I can further rely on biblical reference to support my initial premise. I must also highlight that nullifying the idea that one race is naturally superior applies to all races. Objectively speaking, it is certainly possible and most probable that different people within different races can account for greater achievement in specific areas of interest and exposure and as has been suggested proclivities. However, extrapolating from Dr. Constance's description, there is no biblical evidence to support the proposition that one's ethnicity offers a natural advantage when mental capacity is considered. Physical traits, however, may indicate that inherited height may be advantageous in certain categories of sports or employment. On the other hand, groups of people who have generally smaller frames have advantages in other endeavors. Sometimes groups or families that represent more robust bodies have advantages over others that are of a more delicate frame. As discussed previously, there are certain talents and gifts which may be displayed among individuals within any race. Certain talents may appear among a family group or gene.

In *A Comprehensive Compilation of Reasons and Strategies to Keep Black Boys Out of Special Education* by author Kawanza Kunjufu, some educators and politicians disregarded his work as chauvinistic, even biased because of his emphasis of black boys. However, a fair reading of the material would clarify that Mr. Kunjufu's evidence and outline was clearly needed. Black boys in the 1980s were disproportionately represented in special education programs in schools across the country. Frequently, these boys who may have demonstrated exceptional potential in primary grades qualified for various special services by the 4th grade. Their academic performance remained substandard throughout their high school life. Subsequently, the phenomenon known as the 4th Grade Failure Syndrome gained popularity. However, early in the 1990's, John Hopkins University published additional research. This information reinforced a gloomy picture of children in general entering into public school education programs. John Hopkins research revealed that every student who entered special education programs by the 4th grade saw only 4 exit the program by the 12th grade. This dismal conclusion seemed to apply to black boys exponentially.

Heading toward the stage of completing my doctorate, it was necessary to participate in a couple of graduate level courses in Design of Research in the behavioral sciences. The courses focused on the role of research in behavioral sciences and the purpose of empirical research in behavioral research. The professor expanded on the sober definition that research is a systematic approach to finding answers to questions. There was in depth discussion about the major characteristics of the scientific method:

1) *Reduce a question to its observable component parts and..*
2) *Test possible answers to the questions*

We were reminded that the scientific method provides basic tools for helping to decide which of the possible alternatives answers to questions are the best (in some sense) on the basis of empirical tests. Supposedly, the purpose of empirical research in the behavioral sciences, in broad terms, is to provide answers to questions about behavior using the scientific method.

Since spending time reviewing the information about research in general and empirical research in particular, more questions have been generated than have been answered. Many answers have conflicted with conclusions determined by acceptable research or scientific method. I ask the question, "Why are there disproportionate numbers of minority children within public schools in special education programs in America"? The answer I got was, "because of poverty". An elliptical response, to be for sure and hardly research based. I have been given to understand that the purpose of behavioral research is to describe, predict and control behavior. Normally, the process of empirical research is: ask a question, review theories and past research, derive a hypothesis (a hypothesis is a statement about what is expected to happen in an experiment), and design a study in order to collect data (information) bearing on the hypothesis. At the appropriate place and time, statistics set forth guidelines for summarizing and describing data. The statistics provide methods for drawing inferences from groups of subjects to larger groups of people and the statistics set forth guidelines for selecting subjects for a study.

There are generally 3 types of statistics utilized in behavioral research: Descriptive statistics, Inferential statistics and Random Sampling. Their purpose is to provide some kind of picture of what happened in the study. Poverty does not offer much of a picture or explanation for why there is a disproportionate number of minority children in special education in America's public schools.

One term which should be clarified in the question being asked is "disproportionate". The idea surfaces from the acceptance of normal curve equivalents in frequency distribution. This suggests in a distribution of $100, the 100 dollars is distributed equally among four individuals, each receiving $25. Or, the $100 could be equally distributed between two individuals with $50 each. These two examples would both be equal distributions. The second example would be symmetrical: two halves mirror each other.

In many education discussions used to place students based on their intelligence, the normal curve of intelligence is used. It is a type of frequency distribution. The "normal" of intelligence suggests that if a truly random selection of people were conducted within American society, there would generally be four groups of people based on their intelligence. On a distribution of 0-100, the scale would reflect 25% of people in the quadrants, 1-25 (25%), 26-49 (25%, 50-75 (25%), 76-100 (25%). Based upon this theory of normal distribution examination, 1-10 % of the randomly selected individuals would score exceptionally low on an intelligence assessment. However, on the positive side, 1-10% of the individuals would score 90-99, exceptionally high. The largest group, 50-75% of the people would score within the normal range of intelligence.

Objectivity and replication have revealed that uncontrolled variables can affect research results. This reminds scientists that ideas such as the intelligence of human beings can only be framed theoretically to reflect some comparative relationship of one individual or group to another. These theories cannot become the final predictor or indication of any individual's intellectual capacity. That mistake leads to bias favoring familiarity, environments, experiences, language, gender or innumerable other prejudices.

While attending college in the late 1960's and 1970's I shared classes with Vietnam veterans. These men primarily performed better than students fresh out of high school. Aside from natural ability, other factors attributed to the discrepancy. Their maturity perhaps made a contribution. Maturity amplified by world travel and global experience are other considerations. However, I strongly believe that the veterans' intrinsic motivation level accounted for the ability to focus and direct their energy to a realistic end. All of these men were able to benefit from the benefits of the "G.I. Bill", which includes tuition and a stipend for other personal use.

Often, the GPA of the veterans surpassed that of the younger classmates, even when the classmates were the academic elite of the various high schools across the country. We know that these veterans may have experienced and observed horrible scenes of war. For some, those experiences contributed to dysfunction. For many others, they somehow excelled. Perhaps their internal motivation enabled them to compartmentalize mental distractions. Instead of distracting their memories, it enabled them to utilize their past to fuel their expectations for the future they envisioned. I need to note that frequently the veterans, chronologically, were significantly older than some of the other college students. However, they seemed to expect more or required less academic support or external motivation from the college environment. However, that level of independence and self -reliance can be cultivated among students at any level. Institutions or motivation sources are needed to help students learn how to complete tasks motivated by their own decision making or judgement.

NOT A RESPECTER OF PERSONS

This debate regarding supremacy of one race over another will undoubtedly persist. My question to Christians remains, "Is there a biblical clarification which supports why many students of certain races in our country land into special education programs?". In some predominantly minority schools, the representation of minority children ranges up to 90% of the special education population. This ratio exists even when the students compose of 10-15% of the total student population.

It has been reported that this disproportionate representation of brown and black students in special education is due to the high rate of poverty among their communities. This would be a disturbing indictment on the educational system in our country, if the latter were true. However, we should remember that, except for critical injury or sickness, intelligence does not decrease over time. Yet, the percentage of minority special education classification increases exponentially each year. If poverty is the culprit, there is still a serious problem which can and should be corrected. Otherwise, our country is allowing thousands of lives to be wasted away because of the lack of food or other essentials. From a Christian perspective, a greater deficit is being perpetrated. Hundreds of people created with amazing ability and divine purpose are unable to fulfill their destinies because we deprive them of support. We may be guilty of undermining God's purposes in this world. Though human beings cannot thwart God's plans, we can interfere and reap the negative consequences.

Ephesians 2:10 reassure young people, *"For we are God's handiwork created in Christ Jesus to do good works, which God prepared in advance for us to do"*. These considerations are addressed to Believers. It is necessary to repeat that fact. It is expressed with the expectation that the idea will be examined with a spiritual yet critical eye. Special education is one area which, as an educator, troubles my understanding of God and His relationship with His human creation. The concepts of divine love, divine justice and divine compassion clash precipitously with the reality reflected in our country regarding our young people. The inequity and inequality are stark among young people living in the same country. I am not advocating socialism where all people experience the same resources, etc. regardless of their efforts or investment. Instead, I protest that a disservice exists when all children attending a publicly funded institution are treated distinctly differently with no credible rationale, especially when these differences influence the rest of their lives.

Young people, if they are going to invest time and effort to succeed academically, must be persuaded that the cards are fair and not stacked against them in their communities and their schools. Differences which arise out of uncontrolled circumstances or situations can be made level by an all powerful God. Zechariah 12:1-2 says, *"The Lord who stretches out heaven, who lays the foundation of the earth and who forms the human spirit within a person declares"*:

1) *Does one God create all?*
2) *WIll one God who creates all provide blessings and advantage for one person only forever or one people eternally?*
3) *If so, then is He yet a God who is not a respecter of persons in blessing or punishment?*

What then is taking place? Why are many children of color performing exponentially lower academically on standardized assessments than people in the majority race? We should acknowledge that in American public schools, many children of Asian descent achieve quite well, particularly in mathematics and the sciences. In fact, these are disciplines, quite frequent, where Asian American young people surpass most other ethnic groups. The academic malaise which seems to affect Native American, Latino and African American students is frequently noted in the experience of Asian American students. The discussions related to low academic performance of black and brown students have surfaced often over the decades. However, recently educators particularly have inclined believing that the low performance among these students correlated with their environment. There is also limited research that suggests that a young person's exposure to certain kinds of life experiences can influence the academic performance of individuals. American history records questionable research concluding that genetics contributes solely to the inferiority of certain races and their performance.

Ibram X. Kendi's,"Stamped from the Beginning, the Definitive History of Racist Ideas in America ", traces many of the racist ideas, assimilationist compromises and segregationist suppositions. These notions have been accepted and served as the foundation of state and federal laws designed to perpetuate questionable ideologies even though these hereditary propositions have been debunked on numerous occasions. The prevailing fallacy emanated from such research was that there is indeed one supreme race of people. Therefore, all other races should expect to experience sub performance when compared to the superior group.

However, the consideration for 21st century Christians is the differences in academic performance of students attributable to forces in the environment or rooted in inferior creations. If the cases are environmental, many schools are victimizing under-privileged students. If the discrepancy is attributed to genetics, we are perpetrating an untruth if we espouse that all children can learn. These questions should be answered. Christians who propose a God who created all things and said that "It is good" have a critical responsibility to themselves and their faith.

There is a challenge facing all who agree with what is needed to alter the way that some young people think and behave. We have talked about what the adults should introduce these young people to. The truth is that if they understand the beauty of their creation and unique purpose, their behavior should coincide. Unfortunately, many of us understand that there may be an absence of adult voices to convey the message. Another difficult reality is that many youth may not access a book like this or attend a gathering where similar ideas will be discussed. Young people will observe examples of people who may apply principles in their lives and still fail. They may see people who experience a catastrophic injury or illness. An illness even at birth which renders them totally dependent on medical assistance for survival. That individual will never be able to complete or demonstrate academic competence. In these instances, young people must be reminded that there are exceptions which exist. We do not know why God allows such things. We have to be honest with youngsters. God is sovereign.

The premise about a sovereign God is based primarily on what is recorded in the Bible, King James Version. This version is supposedly based on the accumulation of evidence reflected in the dead sea scrolls and religious testimony and interpretation. These interpretations are accepted as inerrant, God inspired. At some point each believer must determine his level of confidence in the reliability of the Bible. Can a person openly defend a composition whose validity is questionable? This writer could not. The process required me to enter into a serious quest for information which could be challenged outside of a religious context and still maintain its credibility. My conclusion enabled me to ignore unfounded allegations or theories which were not supported by what I read. My conclusions provoked me to question the God of the Bible about His consistency and His existence. I received the assurance I sought. Now I Do NOT have to stretch what I accept as truth in order for it to comply with my political preferences or biases.

In my search for the truth, my personal experience with God, who I currently trust, enables me to establish consistency about how I live as well as how I accept other created beings. I have read the Bible in its entirety several times. As a composite whole, there is nothing which supports the idea that anyone should view any other human being more or less than oneself. It also does not propose that one person should think more highly of another individual based on the color of their skin or pedigree. Such a perception would divest me of the faith and confidence my salvation rests on. The God of justice and compassion would cease to exist for me.

At the risk of sounding judgmental, a tremendous level of personal dissonance resonates in my spirit when I hear professing Believers who claim to love and trust a God who is just, while they discriminate against another human being created in His image. Proverbs 16:21-24 expresses, *"The wise in heart shall be called prudent and the sweetness of the lips increaseth in learning. Understanding is a wellspring of life unto him that hath it"*. Our genuine Christian Believers advocate that human beings of a darker hue are inferior to those who are lighter, emanating from an Anglo-Saxon heredity.

Regardless of its longevity and popularity, many people still question the integrity of the Bible. Believers who propose and support the concept that created individuals of Anglo-Saxon heritage are designed at a level of superior intellect and creativity proposes at least a mathematically improbability. This is especially since the percentage of non Anglican descendants greatly outnumber those of Anglican heritage.

Another disconcerting existence is the effort that the smaller human population of the world invest inordinate amounts of time and efforts attempting to convince the majority population that the former is superior. Laws, policies, economic and governmental structures have been created to propagate the control of the supposedly weaker dependent subgroup of the world. This is difficult to rationalize with an objective framework.

This chapter of the book was not originally intended to be a Christian expose, even though yours truly is a professing believer and retired educator. This is intended to be a protest against continuing placement of children of color and low socioeconomic students into special education programs. Too often, the success of the programs may be measured by the job security it provides for staff and meager supplemental income to parents of the children. Unfortunately, often these parents are not fully aware of the long term devastation their compliance has on the placement of their children into these programs.

The essential question of this chapter is, Why label these children initially? If there is a possibility or probability that all children are created equally, why are the children being overwhelmed with monikers or descriptions depicting inferiority or insufficiency? There is no Biblical support for these designations.

Let us review additional scripture references pertaining to God's decision about destiny. In Judges 12:5-6, the scripture talks about the survivors of the battle between Ephraim and Gilead. The survivors of Gilead controlled the Jordan River that the survivors of Gilead wanted to cross over. The Gileadites could not recognize the survivors of Ephraim from their physical appearance. However, the Ephraims apparently possessed a cultural or dialectal speech distinction. The Giladites devised a test for anyone who was their enemy, the Ephraimites. Before anyone was allowed to cross the river, they had to pronounce the Shibboleth. Unfortunately, the Ephraimites pronounced the word as "Shibboleth", eliminating the "sh" sound.

Their inability led to death and the seizure of any Ephraimite. Their inability to verbalize "sh" was either a learned cultural or language peculiarity. Perhaps, similar to the reputable Bostonian tendencies to blend "ar" into "ah", the word car sounds like "kah". These distinctive pronunciations are not criticized by the general American public. Instead, the Bostonian pronunciations are envied as New England elegance. This difference does not imply inferior intelligence of the people from that New England region.

Another example is found in Judges 13:4-5. This scripture references how Samson, as a child, was dedicated to God from the womb. His mission was to take the lead in delivering the Israelites from Philistine domination. Is there universal agreement among Bible believers that every child is dedicated to God from their womb? Obviously, once delivered from the womb, the environment influences the child's development. Even with Samson's divine call, his proclivities and associations attributed to his demise. Behavior and unwise choice should not necessarily destine an individual to failure with no hope of redemption. By the end of Samson's life, following bouts of drunkenness and ultimate physical blindness, his testimony is that he killed more enemies in his death than at any time when he was alive. Samson was a unique individual with many flaws, yet his ability was unquestionable.

A similar example in Luke 1:1 rings true, the birth of John the Baptist is hailed as a miraculous event, partially because of his mother's advanced age. An angel announced the miracle to John's father, Zachariah. Zachariah was anointed with a song. The song testifies about the person for which his son was born, "My child will be called a prophet. He will go on before the Lord to prepare the way, to give his people knowledge of salvation". Another special circumstance of John's birth was the angel outlining special instructions on how his parents were to rear him,

Samson's parents and John's parents experienced similar miraculous encounters with angels surrounding the births. Samson's mother was alone when the angel informed her about her son's imminent birth. Her husband, Manoah, was so astounded and concerned that he asked God for the angel to return to teach his wife and himself how to rear the child (Judges 13: 6-7). Then in Judges 13:12, Menorah and his wife asked the angels if there were any specific rules they needed in order to govern their son's life and work. In Judges 20: 24-25, "The woman gave birth. He grew and the Lord blessed him".

Perhaps, many of us who are or have been parents wish directions could have been provided to grow their children's life and work. The truth of the matter is that God has provided some rules to help rear their children so that they can prepare for their lives and life's work. Sadly, these directions are not always readily available in schools or homes where children are found. Unfortunately, even when the rules in the book are present in the home, too often the Bible is not researched for directions. Adults who interact with children outside of the home are frequently placed in difficult positions. This is especially true for professionals like teachers. It is difficult to teach a child who resists following any rules for his or her life. Children with such an uncooperative attitude may never obtain an understanding of what to do with their lives or life's work. Some of these young people are having negative labels placed on them because of their misbehavior. These references are inaccurate and unintentionally dishonest. Behavior is a tragic justification to permanently undermine a young person's potential. Accurate policies and practices which indicate effective strategies are needed to address the authentic behavior problem.

In Judges 20:16, there is a description of a special group of Benjamites. They are preparing to fight the Israelites.." *Among the soldiers there were seven hundred select troops who were left handed, each of them could sling a stone at a hair's breath and not miss"*. In numerous instances, the Bible describes individuals or groups of individuals gifted with special talents. Often, these special attributes were provided by God for special occasions.

During Israel's exodus, God commanded Moses to build a tabernacle. The design was very definitive, as were the materials to be used for the construction. God directed Moses to have the people bring gold, silver, bronze, blue, purple and scarlet yarn, fine linen, goat hair, ram skins dyed red and another type of durable leather. He also requested acacia wood, olive oil for light, spices for the anointing oil and the fragrant incense, onyx stones and other gems to be mounted on the ephod and breastplate. The list of materials was extensive. However, a significant aspect of the construction process for the tabernacle was that God told Moses about the clothing for the priest and building for the tabernacle. God commanded, *"Every skilled woman with her hands brought and spun blue, purple or scarlet yarn and fine linen and All the women who were willing and had the skill to spin goat hair"*. Then in Exodus 35:30-35, Moses conveys to the Israelite congregation…" *The Lord has chosen Bezalel, son of Uri, the son of Hur…and has filled him with the spirit of God with wisdom, with understanding, with knowledge and with all kinds of skills to make artistic designs for the work in gold, silver and bronze…to cut and set stones, to work and engage in all kinds of artistic crafts, and has given both him and Oholiab the ability to teach others. He (God) has filled him with skill to do all kinds of work as engravers, designers, embroiderers…all of the skilled workers"*.

God's knowledge and wisdom are extensive. It is advisable to remember that the human race, male and female, are created in His image. Therefore, I question if it is rational for any individual emanating from one common mind, should dictate by opinion or other critical means, the capability of another human being. As believers, it is critical that we consider this practice, especially as it is applied in education. Imperfect assessment tools are utilized to restrict many students from particular cultures from achieving their full potential. Instead, these students are neglected to mediocrity and low expectations because they failed to comply with someone's biased perspective. They eagerly assign labels of incompetence rather than recognizing a performance which is unmotivated. Unfortunately, students as young as four years old are designated in need of special support services, even though cultural and environmental practices of expectation may stimulate entirely different physical and cognitive maturation levels. A child's artistic skills inherited in his or her DNA may be labeled "easily distracted". Another musical prodigy may see music notes in his mind and feels rhythm in his hands and feet. He is labeled "attention deficit" because he has trouble maintaining focus on one letter alphabet and demonstrates inability to remain still.

It is curious how many young people would verbalize the idea, "Why are you labeling me?". Help me be what I was created to be. Let me dream, let me dance. Let me laugh, may I help others laugh? Let me draw. I might utilize mathematics to measure my architectural creation or musical refrain. I might use words to describe the shapes and colors of my paintings. I will build houses, write poems, disassemble the atom again or reattach broken femurs and ankles. I might utilize symbols to compose prescriptions and movie scores. These children may one day scream, "Why do you keep labeling me!". I am different so you grown people must prepare me to accept, nurture and cultivate that difference. God said, "And He saw that it was good". So Christian believer, "Why are you still labeling me? I am like you. I am you, created in His likeness. Can you accept you and not accept me?". A life script exists in a label.

Young people should be able to access important guidance from the adults associated with a healthy Christian church. Burgeoning individuals may be uncertain about what their Creator has in store for them. They may require assistance in understanding His written word or the messages generated through the Holy Spirit. Their confidence must be cultivated by guidance and personal experiences. God's written word will achieve clarity and meaning. Young people will learn to trust the written word as it applies to their lives. That trust will store confidence in their own capability towards any challenge in life. They will be able to step boldly into any circumstance with coverage and assurance.

A certain question lingers. Theoretically, if intellectual potential among human beings is distributed proportionally among all groups of people, why are so many young people from certain subgroups appearing disproportionately in education programs for low academic performance? The answer to this question is complex and controversial. It is possible that there are too many students inappropriately placed in special education programs across the country. Our country has created numerous descriptors which classify students. Some of these descriptions have questionable medical or scientific support. Believers should be among the first and loudest voices questioning this discrepancy in the number and color of certain children purportedly requiring the aforementioned services. If God creates all things, does that picture square with biblical history or concepts. You people must be informed that they must accept responsibility when that responsibility is clearly on their shoulders.

Intelligence does not decrease overtime except for certain medical conditions including, brain injury or disease. Yet, many individuals who demonstrate exceptional talent and intellect in preschool and primary school are found in special education programs by third, fourth or fifth grades. It is not difficult to deduce how financial conditions of parents or exposure benefit many children and cripple others. There may be other less scholarly considerations which negatively impact children and their mental progress. Adult expectations may be more important than the recognition it is provided. The low expectations for the academic success for certain young people may contribute to on-going low academic performance and waste of potential in our education institutions and society.

Adults can and must communicate to young people that individual effort and attitude can impact one's success. However, they should also be informed that there are young people equal to them in every respect except they are challenged with overcoming negative environmental factors in school and home. Therefore, judgement of some people may be unfair; unless we have walked in their shoes.

God has provided within each person the intelligence or gifts needed to fulfill their purpose in the world. However, some individuals may have to struggle harder to overcome environmental obstacles. Adult believers should advocate that no, God is no respecter of persons". He has not favored any individual or racial group with intellect or gifts above another. A search history will confirm that among all living persons and their recent ancestors exist intellectual artistic histories and documents with rich culture, creativity and economic advancements. Many of these cultures existed long before our current European based value systems and centuries ahead of the Judeo-Christian principles, which modern believers testify. Having an understanding of this history should remind Christian believers that the history of man reveals an alternating existence of powerful empires over hundreds of years. There is a record of various races and ethnicities which dominated the then known world economy and politics. Sometimes, the power was shared among the most powerful empire, politically. Yet, the preeminence was not dictated by skin color or ethnic ancestry. That bias based on physical attributes is a relatively modern concept.

If young people are going to be persuaded that their opportunities to succeed in this world are equitable because their Creator is not a respecter of persons, adults must advocate and demonstrate their acceptance of that truth. Parents or surrogate parents must help young people to develop self -confidence. The young people must have confidence that they can learn anything that aligns with their God given purpose. They must understand and accept that as a created being, their responsibility is to demonstrate excellence, excellence in academic achievement and any other endeavor. This attitude must be adopted as the mantra for their lives. They can absorb their creator's words regarding their existence (Psalm 139: 13-14):

"For You created my innermost being, You knit me together in my mother's womb. I praise you because I am fearfully and wonderfully made; Your works are wonderful. I know that full well".

The testimony of the Psalmist is that there is no fault in what God has created. Everything is for a purpose, perfectly designed to accomplish the purpose. If there is a short fall, the weakness is not in God's creation. The impairment is elsewhere. All have been created for different purposes, therefore various strengths and talents may represent the diversified purposes. However, if a disproportionate number of God's creation implies misalignment with God's purpose by human estimation, it is time for the human factor to re-examine its vision or interpretation of God's purpose.

Increasingly large amounts of human misalignment with God's word is unbiblical. It is time to review the Word of God and measure everything else against it. Only then should we feel comfortable proceeding in the current direction. So many young people in the present society are confused, frustrated, angry and afraid. They articulate their doubt about the existence of any future, some resign themselves to a life of negativity and conflict. Many are unhappy. They have little or no confidence in adults or the God some adults talk about. They are dangerous to themselves and to others. They have little self value and the value they hold for others is less.

Adults must help young people. The critical responsibility adults have is to help young people be all they are created to be. To find out about that purpose, adults must read the manual, The Bible. When youngsters are born, they have already been God approved. Our job is to follow the guide, follow the directions. Occasionally, like any entity of valuable adjustments may be required. However, things still seem out of order, read the manual again. There is frequently something we missed. If we refuse to read the manual, even though things are not working out, we need to stop complaining. The Creator has the answers. Adults can help young people if we put in the time to find out what our ordained purpose is. Read the manual. Help the youngster be all they were created to be. You will find in the midst of conflict, human catastrophe and pain, God still does all things well.

HELP ME BECOME ...
ALL I WAS CREATED TO BE...

The term "youth" encompasses a broad description of individuals. The term may even acquire various connotations depending on one's geographical location. In North America, "youth" generally refers to individuals below voting age, too young to legally buy alcohol or enlist in a voluntary army. In Southeast Asia, youth may denote an age extremely different. Young girls may be encouraged to prepare for marriage before their 15th birthday. I have to qualify. My perspective is toward the United State's culture, where youth is appropriate to individuals who have not attained to 21 years of age. In Reclaiming Our Youth, I referenced the term "reclaim" by definition. I concluded that the term means "to take back". I alluded to the fact that when the word is used in the active voice, it not only expresses action, which is initiated, but simultaneously conveys a reaction. The person who is reacting illustrates his or her possession at a former time. This is a riveting reality. As unoriginal as it sounds, it is a contradiction to reclaim something of which one never possessed control. I further clarified in my earlier discourse that possession was synonymous with the word "influence". It is the influence over our youth which is the challenge.

Of this discussion, this idea is presented in the current context as well as parents or surrogate parents, it is critical to establish influence over our children. There has to exist a response from them of respect toward us as adults. It does not require adults to hover and establish total dominance over their children's actions and thinking. It does require that our youth recognize us as a voice in their daily interactions, which demand us to be heard and responded to. Unfortunately, if that influence has never been established and reinforced, there is little opportunity to cultivate that relationship when the youth is older or under the influence of other forces, other people or circumstances.

I reflect on numerous situations where I heard parents exclaim, "I just don't know what to do with that child, He/she does not listen! ". This discussion is promoted as a Christian based perspective, however, minus the existence of appropriate views the youth maintains toward legal authority. Framing this in a spiritual context is insufficient to make a real difference. I am not conceding that youth who do not recognize authority at home will find little success complying with limitations outside of their home, short of physical force. Sadly, influence acquired by force is rarely sustained for a meaningful period of time.

I believe that healthy influence over our children can be established, maintained and even reclaimed. The process of reclaiming is much more complex and requires clear commitment from both parents and the children. In many circumstances, support from a strong, well organized spiritual institution may be able to help. However, the assistance expected from a spiritual institution might come with the expectation that the parents show up consistently so that the effort reflects team work. The youth will probably become familiar with biblical ideas such as, "Children obey your parents in the Lord for this is right (Ephesians 6:1)", or "honor your father and your mother that your days may be long ...(Exodus 20:12)".

I believe that domestic conflicts, as well as many conflicts with youth and legitimate authority outside of the house have a spiritual origin. Parents who regularly expose themselves to spiritual ideas such as, "Fathers, provoke not your children to wrath (Ephesians 6:4). What parents will realize at some point is that the wisdom and stamina that is needed to establish and maintain some positive influence over their children is through the help of the only wise God. This is not a guarantee that all relationship conflicts will be resolved but it certainly increases the odds in your favor.

Earlier, I referred to parents or surrogates in this modern time. That surrogate may be grandparents, aunts, uncles or foster parents who are at the center of the relationship with a child. As discussions take place and strategies are considered to address the issue of influence over a child, several topics need to be reviewed. One question is, has anyone ever had influence over the child? A second question for consideration is, when was the influence lost and, if possible, why? How did the child behave when someone had influence? What does the child look like when no one has control or influence over them? Another set of questions that may be useful are:

- *What is the observable descriptor in the relationship we desire to have with the children?*
- *How will the relationship be different when the child is under your influence?*
- *What is the timeframe of the process to bring about the changes?*
- *What are the steps and goals?*
- *What benchmarks of behavior will help you know if you are headed in the right direction?*

By various standards, there is general agreement among observers and individuals affected by unchecked behavior that too many parents have lost control or influence over their children. Unfortunately, much of that lack impacts the communities who theseyouth live at or frequent. Frequently, this deficit of positive influence is credited to parents of youth among urban neighborhoods. However, statistically though youth among urban neighborhoods experience a disproportionate amount of adverse consequences relative to their anti-sociable behavior, their number of incidents is lower than youth of more affluent neighborhoods. The explanation for this discrepancy continues to be debated. We will not debate it here. The definitive answer exceeds the scope of our current conversation. The truth of the matter is that, regardless of ethnicity or socio-economic status, one young person demonstrating behavior that imposes and disturbs the life of others is too many. Reasonable self control should be expected of every person, youth or not.

So, what behaviors should parents observe to provide evidence that their youth are developing appropriately in a socially established culture? The following list will center around psychopathic behaviors identified in Magid and McKelvey's book, <u>High Risk: Children Without a Conscience</u> (1988).

1) *Do not demonstrate hatred towards others*
2) *Refrain from intentionally hurting others*
3) *Exemplify remorse if they injure or accidentally kill another person*
4) *They are not arrogant*
5) *They possess shame at appropriate times*
6) *They demonstrate a level or morality*
7) *They are not impulsive*
8) *They are sociable*
9) *They are not superficial*
10) *They are not callous*
11) *They are responsible*
12) *They are reverent, with a genuine respect for other people's value, beliefs and property*

Even though this is a faith based monograph, I have attempted to identify behavior attributes which can and perhaps should exist beyond a faith based environment. These expectations are hopefully global in nature. Parents from a broad range of settings would be pleased if their own children's behavior is consistent with the examples prescribed.

The title of this book is, <u>All Things Well</u>. The implication refers to the truth that God does all things well and that He is no respecter of persons in terms of discipline or blessings. I proceed with this discussion based on the premise that all Christians believe this about God. Clearly, though the premise may be true, we understand that all youth are not Christians, neither are their parents. Yet, the non-Christian parents desire similar behavior from their children. As they would welcome interacting with other children who behave in positive ways, we also confess that even the most disciplined youth reared in consistently Christian homes, do not display virtuous behavior always. So, where do we go from here?

Step one is to understand that all of our children, from birth, possess the same proclivities toward evil and psychopathological behavior. "We have all fallen short. (Romans)". Also, "Evil is bound up in the heart of a child (Proverbs)". Essentially, there should be no surprise when most children lean to behavior which is antisocial and callous. Some might question, "If God does all things well, why are some children less anti-sociable"? Perhaps some of these differences can be accounted for based on specific inherited personality traits which may tend one toward less antisocial behavior. Home environment, training or parental expectations established very early may also account for the differences. Those differences do not nullify the truth that by nature, all of us are similar.

So, as parents, if we want our children to behave appropriately, it requires some effort on our parents and exposure. The exposure will be to God's Word. The same book which teaches control of children also teaches fathers to not drive your children to wrath and break their spirit. It teaches husbands to love their wives and that children are a blessing from the Lord, so we should treasure them and care for them. It also teaches children to obey their parents, for this is right and it reminds youth that if they want to have a long life, they should honor their fathers and mothers.

Step 2 of the process of managing and manipulating the behavior of our youth is exposure to the Holy Spirit. That is done by providing an opportunity for them to come to a saving knowledge of Jesus Christ. The tendency we all have toward antisocial behavior can only be continuously battled by the Holy Spirit who can initiate right thinking and right behavior at home and abroad. To be honest, we are not talking about creating perfect people, young or old. We are attempting, with God's help, to rear young people who will positively influence their surroundings as opposed to terrorizing and destroying themselves and their community.

Step 3 of the process is to influence the behavior of our youth with parental involvement, parental support and parental example. I used to believe that parent involvement or parental support would suffice. I have learned better. Parental involvement is parents taking their youth where the support is. Parents who send their young people to church or another type of institution, need to go with them. You have to let them see that you are serious about it. You also need to hear some of the things that the young people are hearing. If it is good for them, then it should be good for you. Otherwise parents, you will appear hypocritical.

Parents, you demonstrate support when you demonstrate that you are holding yourself accountable for how you interact with your youth as much as you hold them accountable to how they interact with you. Then, of course, setting an example of what you want to see is important. There is such a thin line between providing support and setting an example that if we focus well on one or the other, we will surely cover them both. Nevertheless, I am assured that if God's Word is applied at a gut level, your effort will tremendously reduce the destructive behavior observed among some of our young people. To some people, the aforementioned suggestions may appear simplistic, even naive. Yet, in many cases, counseling has been implemented, harsh punishment and deprivation has been implemented, even short or long term incarceration have risen. Yet, the problems have not diminished.

I have been frequently reminded that if I continue to assemble a mechanical device without success, read the instructions. I highly recommend that for the sake of our youth in the 21st century somebody needs to read the instructional manual. "In the beginning, God created..."(Genesis 1:1) Or"... call unto me and I will answer you and tell you great and unsearchable things you do not know..." (Jeremiah 33:3).

Before adults can help the youth, they must recognize their responsibility to the ultimate authority of the universe. This is part of the true essence of helping the youth. Adults must recognize and remember their accountability to God, "Children are a gift from the Lord". The accountability to God for the sake of the youth applies to all adults who have significant impact on the young person's life (educators, ministers, youth leaders, secular or spiritual). Additionally, it is our responsibility to set an example for the youth. If we do not demonstrate a level of reverence, the youth by large will follow our example. Once we understand the divine connection we have, we can help guide the youth in recognizing their divine connection as well.

I realize that thousands of adults and young people protest that they are fine and do well without embedding any spiritual considerations into their lives. That is, if their success is measured by material success as a result of a good education, political connections or even talents. I do not propose that in order for youth to acquire material success, they must be spiritual or read the bible. Obviously, that is a false conclusion, however, unless we consider that success supersedes mere material achievement. If we postulate that "good success" (Joshua 1:7-8) includes fulfillment, peace of mind, acknowledgement that you have completed the task that you were created for and for which we're most suited (mentally, spiritually and physically), success takes on a more visceral expectation.

The question of why I am here has a thorough explanation. How many times do the media account for individuals who take their lives, leaving behind a surplus of money, houses and land that seemingly had little value to the victim? There are exceptions of course. There appears to be individuals who appear to have it all: material success and an enjoyable life without seeming invested in their spiritual potential. However, the Bible is either true or not. Its inerrancy must be shown by the consistency we can observe in people's lives, not the exceptions. This position does not conclude that those who adhere to spiritual teaching and living will never experience any difficulties. Nevertheless, good success is God's Word. Obedience places the primary responsibility on Him to fulfill His promise. That in itself is satisfying. God is faithful. The Word of God is true and powerful. Therefore, faith and experience confirm that if we apply the principles of God's Word, the results are going to be positive, regardless of circumstance.

I believe that the overriding task that we as parents must confront is helping our youth become all that God has created them to be. This should be what youth can expect from the adults in their lives who care about them. Young people should articulate, "If I am created by God for a special purpose, why don't you help me be all that I am created to be". This should not be viewed as a question. Instead, it must be a request; perhaps a demand. Parents will need to prepare a definitive, clear plan to carry out their plan. They need to accept the responsibility of what they want to do for their youth. When will the process begin and how long will it persist? A decision or discussion needs to occur to clarify if the youth will be forced to accept certain values which align with the character development that we want to see? Do parents insist that their charge demonstrates certain attitudes? Should parents demand that the behavior of their youth align with specific expectations that we possess? These are some questions for consideration as parents accept the challenge of supporting their youth.

References have been to God, creation and the Bible. As such, the discussion has transitioned into a spiritual realm. Individuals who discount the existence or significance of spiritual relevance in the lives of young people will not be receptive to the content of this book. I concede to the loss of a significant potential readership. I contest that a lack of spiritual acknowledgement does not nullify the latter's existence in the lives of youth.

Nevertheless, before the adults can support their youth on their journey to fulfillment and spiritual completeness, we must understand and accept our own relationship with the Creator, God. We cannot lead others where we do not go. Prior to helping our youth, we must have enlisted in the spiritual battle that our youth will engage in. We need to be unequivocally clear. This will be a war waged against the forces of evil; an evil which is as real as the benevolent God from whom we seek guidance and protection. Evil is indeed the antagonist. Our children are the spoils. When evil wins, our children lose. There is no more devastating truth than the adage, "To the victor goes the spoils". The loss of potential dreams and gifts to the world may vanish because a precious child was unable to become what he or she was created to be destined to do.

In order to help prepare our youth to participate in the battle against evil, the adults must help feed them nourishing food and expose them to experiences which will increase their awareness and resistance to people, places and things designed for their destruction. Many young people today interact with electronic games of contests which challenge their mental acuity and manual dexterity. These kinds of activities familiarize them with the concept of winning, losing and consequences. In their personal realities, they must understand that losing may cost them their entire future. The wonderful future that their Creator designed for them can be annulled by unwise decisions or counterproductive behavior.

To help prepare our youth against the destructive elements which exist in some environments, there are some steps that parents can take. The first step is to train our youth. This explanation may sound exceptionally secular but there are some points for consideration. A professor, Dr, Morris E. Massey, developed a thought provoking lecture titled, What You Are is. Where You Were. When You Were Value Programmed. There are several ideas that he proposes. His concept about value programming is that every human being is taught through word, action or deed to value certain things or people and to not value other things and people. Developed over time, attitudes towards categories of ideas, persons, places and things become part of a value system through which everything in a person's life is filtered. As experiences are screened through this value system, they are labeled valuable-important or not valuable-not important. Subsequently, in terms of opinions and attitudes, experiences, ideas or people that enter into an individual's psyche are reacted to based upon the "label" that he or she has attached to it.

For example, an individual's attitude towards black people, white people, short people, tall people, thin people or portly people has been influenced by his or her value system. Other entities which may stimulate a reaction based on one's value system include extramarital affairs, premarital sex, eating habits, money, marriage and interracial dating. The list is in no way exhaustive. The possibilities are as varied and numerous as the people and experiences they have had.

Another factor regarding value programming is that it occurs very early in the life of an individual. Many psychologists who ascribe to this idea advocate that it occurs intentionally or unintentionally early in an individual's life, reportedly between birth and five years of age. Some suggest that it occurs within a different span of time. They generally agree that the process occurs very early in a child's existence. The common thought is that our attitudes about other people, ideas and behaviors are developed during the formative years. The Bible expresses the concept this way, "Train up a child in the way it should go and when he is old, he will not depart from it'. Ephesians 6:4 says, "Bring them up in the training and instruction of the Lord". As parents, we need to remain vigilant that our youth will not always be under our protection from the evil influence of the worldly systems of thinking and behavior. We have to teach and train them to recognize evil temptations and help them develop skills that they can use to make as many wise choices as possible. I repeat, we have to train our youth. The Bible, in Ephesians, indicates that is the father's duty. However, it is not unusual for a mother or other females to assume that responsibility. The important thing is that their children receive training to defend themselves in a spiritual battle that they will face. If the adults do not train them, we are likely placing them on an altar to be sacrificed by evil which will show them no compassion or mercy. Instead, deception will be utilized to draw out the future and smother their dreams. Our youth must be trained.

As we train our youth, we must remain cognizant of maintaining consistency in our own behavior. The following statements generate untold conflict within my own mind, but I am compelled to express that some young people who get trained with adults who sustain a position of influence over them may or may not darken the doors of some of our local churches. Unfortunately, some of our worship centers lack either the focus or insight of helping youngsters discover their true purpose in God. There is a comfort level with providing Summer Vacation Bible School, sports programs or harvest festivals so that they remain occupied and entertained. The realization that business does not equate to spirituality appears to have escaped their understanding. The church must remain focused on targeting spiritual growth by helping young people obtain a serious experience with their Creator. The activities can certainly be an addition, entertainment as a goal is a waste of time. Hearts and minds remain unchanged. Subsequently, parents can not rely solely on a church or any institution to be responsible for "bringing up the child". That is clearly a parent's responsibility. The church can merely provide a safe setting where spiritual principles and concepts may be reinforced or tested for their validity.

I was to provide additional explanation regarding valuing programming and how parents can and should be aware of the ideas being instilled and imprinted into the psyche of their children very early.

Value programs are often heavily influenced by historical events that occur during a person's formative years. For example, an individual reared during a time such as the Great Depression of the 1930's might have specific attitudes regarding the use of money. As an adult, the person might demonstrate strong inclinations to save as much money as possible. On the other hand, someone whose childhood reflected a surplus of money and other material advantages might live an adult life with a much more cavalier attitude toward money.

A change in attitude can be affected if either individual experiences a highly emotional significant event. Let us look at another example related to the phenomenon of value programming. Take, for instance, an individual accustomed to witnessing loyalty in a relatively healthy monogamous relationship, such as marriage. They may take very seriously, not only marriage vows but expect commitment to one person during a dating phase. However, someone exposed to a period of time when a culture promoted more liberal, open relationships might expect less commitment in his or her social relationships. Understanding an individual's family values, personal proclivities and significant emotional events can help anticipate the latter's behavior. This knowledge can help spiritual institutions develop pragmatic activities to reinforce or alter certain social behaviors.

More plainly, there are many different people ingrained with varied beliefs and value systems, rooted in their childhood experience. Parents are advised to be cognizant of the values being instilled in their children. Those values which conflict with what is consistent with the family or community expectations can be attended to; many times prior to them being solidified. Parents are in the position to determine those values which are suitable and right for their children, which are biblical and which are culturally wrong. During the child's formative period, parents can be intentional about utilizing various tools and contrived experiences to reinforce the desired training.

Parents also need to notice the consistency of their lives compared to the expectations for the behavior displayed by the youth. Considerations should provoke questions such as: "Do the youth see examples of acceptable lifestyles in their homes?" and "Can the youth observe the preferred lifestyles in their neighborhoods, city or county?". Truth be told, there is validity in the adage young people believe what adults do, not what they say.

For example, young people may reason: "If the leaders of the country can lie, why can't I?" or "I know adults who cheat on their taxes, so why can't I cheat on a test for a better grade?". They may also think, "I am aware of adults who are unfaithful to their spouses, why shouldn't I be intimate with different partners, especially if I am not married?". The distance between what parents feel as important and what our youth value may be described as a value gap. The ongoing discrepancy creates an atmosphere of dishonesty in the minds of the youth. Parents should attempt strenuously to eliminate the gap. This requires honest, frequent communication between the parent(s) and youth. Being successful at this strategy requires parents to spend time with our youth and develop a healthy relationship with them.

When my children were young, I invested a tremendous amount of time visiting local and state parks. At one stage, the interest of one child drove me to various freshwater and saltwater fishing spots. As a child myself, neither of the recreations appealed to me. Part of my motivation with my children emanated from a range of psychological research that I was exposed to while my children were young. I absorbed some of the theories and operationalized them in my relationship with them. Additionally, I was fortunate that I enormously enjoyed being with my children. However, investing in time with them allowed me to remain somewhat familiar with their social circles as they matured and developed other interests. Many opportunities arose during our visits to fishing holes or lakes to hear their ideas about people, places and things. Some discussions I could enter into immediately without seeming to impose while other topics I made a mental note to divulge into at a later time.

Today, each one of my children are adults with their own families. I am elated to hear about numerous fishing trips they take or their family excursions. All of their recreation is not fishing and parks. Their level of sophistication is much broader than mine was. Now, they are going on family cruises, kayaking, boating or deep sea fishing. Their Facebook posts illustrate some busy lives. I might sense a bit of envy but that momentary remorse is overshadowed by the hugs and laughter they are having with their children. I am encouraged that much sharing of values and beliefs is also transpiring. The parents are building healthy relationships with their children.

Investing time with our youth helps them understand how much they are loved and supported. Being blessed with an executive professional career frequently demands that adults invest an ordinate amount of time to complete certain projects. Frequently, there is a need to work with teams of other professionals, even beyond the walls of the office. Those demands on our time can compete with quality time needed by the youth. Several children psychologists summarized how important it is for our young people to receive reassurance about their value from their parents. I made a commitment to always give my children priority no matter what conversation or project I was engaged in. If my child showed up in the middle of an adult conversation, the conversation paused so that I could give my child my full attention. This method may have appeared rude, it may have been perceived as a father with no influence over his young children. However, my goal was to assure my children that they were valued above anything else. My wife and I agreed that even in our conversations, we would make sure our children, with reasonable guidelines, felt comfortable to interject if they needed to share something they perceived was important. The fact that we gave our children so much of our time unimpeded, the interruptions were rarely needed. This helped to build their self- confidence. They were offered information about possible options. We encouraged them to make their decisions based on the various values and beliefs we had been discussing over the months and years. As parents, we have to accept the reality that our goal in rearing our youth is to help develop youngsters who behave wisely when we, the parents, are not around. When they are able to acknowledge our trust in them, the self -confidence may be stimulated.

We want to help our youth be all they were created to be. Part of this challenge is helping them become comfortable with who they truly are consistent with spiritual principles. They must be comfortable with their gender, no matter what they dislike about it. They must be comfortable with their ethnicity, their race, the color of their skin, texture of their hair, their height and body type. It can become dangerous and utterly miserable when a person spends time attempting to remake himself over and over as culture, styles or other people's opinion's change. This instability can breed frustration or anger with oneself or the world. That kind of mindset may conclude that I am never going to be alright, so why not end this life? This is a conclusion which this country has witnessed too often. The alternative persuasion might conclude that no one is valuable so why not just eliminate as many individuals as possible. Our society has witnessed that destructive behavior also.

With proper training, young people can be taught to be patient and hopeful in favor of adverse economic situations. Biblical principles can help them consider that God may have future opportunities to raise them up to "higher standards". There are hundreds of lives where that possibility has been demonstrated. However, young people can acquire the understanding that even if circumstances are different from what they desire in the present, they do not have to yield to dishonesty or covetousness by using corrupt means to obtain material possessions. Parents must help the young people develop values in which they strive to be true to themselves and the ideals that they have been taught, regardless of possible peer pressure. In Daniel chapter 1, the experience of Zacharias illustrates that appetites must be trained. Parents must teach their young people to draw the line to resist things that fuel their appetites (T.D. Jakes). Bishop Jakes indicates that they must draw a line of confidence, confidence that God's will is perfect. This can only be accomplished when young people have realized their true identity encompassing their created potential, their created purpose and their divine connection. This attitude of life would be the fulfillment of Colossians 3:33. As interpreted in Dr. Stanley's Life Principles Bible, *"Whatever you do, work at it with your heart, as working for the Lord, not for human masters. We must do each task with joy, integrity, diligence and energy because we represent the Lord and others will form their opinions of Him through what they see in us (p. 1697)"*.

Jean Toomer, an African-American writer of the late 20th century, expressed, "Persistent attempts to transcend overt limitations causes one to concentrate on understanding conscience and ability". Mr. Toomer further articulates, "As soon as a person comes to an understanding of himself and understands the rest of the world differently, when he gives birth to hope and forces back a destructive universal perception, it is clear that the expression of his creativity will be represented more clearly and strongly (p.243)".

In another chapter, young people are chastised and reminded that if they believe that a sovereign Creator has provided them with all of the natural abilities and proclivities to successfully fulfill their purpose on earth, they should not be whining, complaining or quitting on life regardless of how difficult it appears. We agree that as adults, parents, surrogates or educators, we should possess a desire to help young people become all that they are created to be. In some instances, the adults in the lives of children must have some idea of how to provide that support. The knowledge of how to provide that support may not be evident. What then are the adults to do? Adults who would be wise should rely on the same source that the young people can rely on for guidance. Ephesians 6:1-3 says, "Children, obey your parents in the Lord, for this is right. Honor your father and mother so that it may go well with you and that you enjoy a long life on the earth". Verse 4 of Esphesians chapter 6 commands, "Fathers, do not exasperate your children, instead bring them up in the training and instruction of the Lord". The source admonishing the young people of behavior which can benefit their lives also reminds parents how to support young people to live blessed lives under the covering of their Creator. Deuteronomy 5:16 is a companion verse to provide guidance to adults for their children. Adhering to a single source of information for parents and children offers consistency. The Bible reminds adults frequently that children are a gift from the Lord. The Lord gives instructions on how to take care of the gift. Regrettably, more than a few instances in our country illustrate the misuse and destruction of special gifts from God. Youngsters are wasting valuable time and potential by failing to make wise choices. Frequently, those unwise choices not only ruin their future but take away their lives through violence or other destructive behavior.

How many adults have been overly excited about a brand new electronic gift, so excited that they toss the manufactured manual aside, relying on our bravo and confidence to enjoy the gift? With nothing happening, all the familiarity of the older model fails to translate into efficiency to operate the new man toy. When pride is subdued and frustration never ends, you end up tossing the gift in a drawer, the same drawer you placed the instructional manual. The five minutes required to pick it up, open it and peruse one page causes an enormous, "Oh! That's how you do it?". You return to the discarded gift and follow the directions. Everything works like a charm. Adults must remember that there is a reason that there are specific directions applied to young people if we really want young people to at least have a chance at operating properly. If we really want them to be all they can be, if we want to help them, we may need to read the manual and stop complaining about the young people. Chances are, there will still be some conflicts or misbehavior. However, the training instilled in them as youngsters will help them recover and refocus when they are older.